I0481811

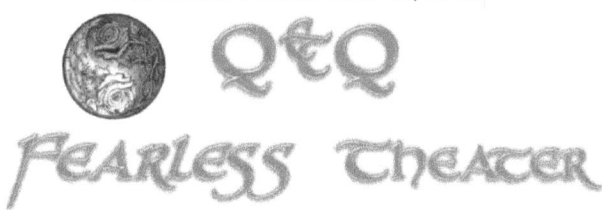

Like Nothing You Have Ever Seen Before

I am so glad to get a chance to talk with you about the Q&Q FEARLESS Theater.

Along with information on our performances, this playbill contains a variety of information:

- Some history on me and how I first found myself doing Live Animation Theater
- Some short bios of Q&Q members
- Some background on our development platform – Second Life
- Some details on the shows we've done
- Some projects we are working on now

Have a look while you settle in to enjoy the show

Jo Karabasz [Rose Artifex]

qqtroupe@gmail.com
www.qqtroupe.org

Contents

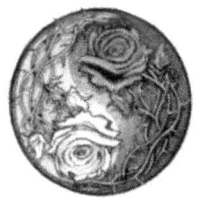

A QUICK INTRODUCTION

The Q&Q FEARLESS Theater is like nothing you've ever seen or heard before. We are a group of artists, technologists, designers, and actors who have been together now for 6 years, working out the ways to marry the incredible 21st century technology of an online development platform to the magic of LIVE classical theatrical performance and create an art form that is as new today as 'moving pictures' were in Edison's time. We perform classic Broadway material, newly written shows, and reworked TV and movies. For each show we "build" a new theater within the development platform called Second Life, and, up until now, our audiences have come there (as avatars) to see us. We produce 2-3 shows a year, and have performed to more than 1000 people each year.

KOWS

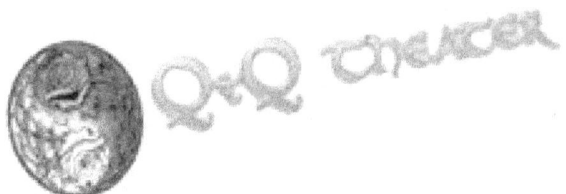

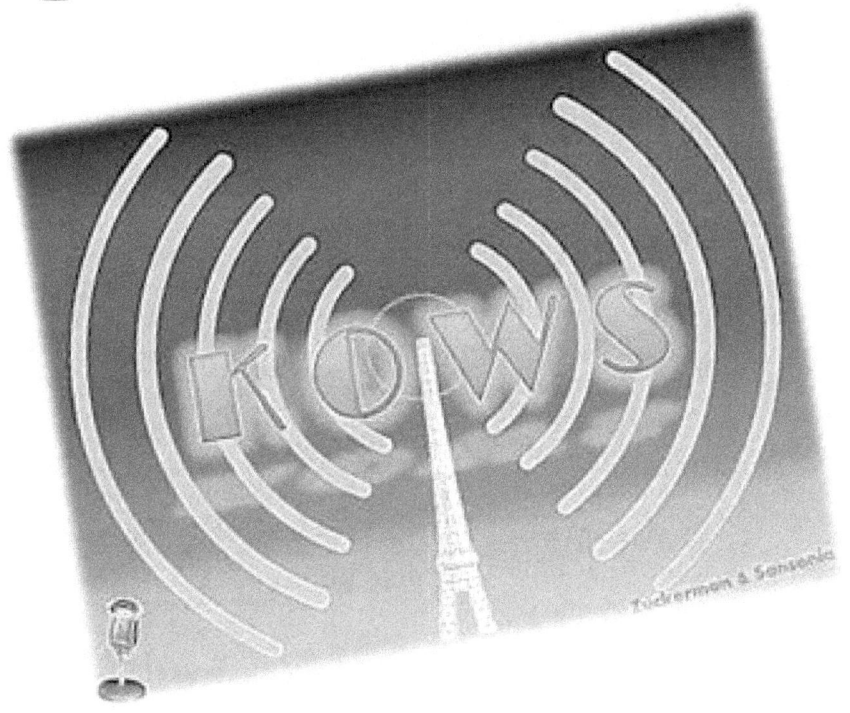

At
http://qqtroupe.org

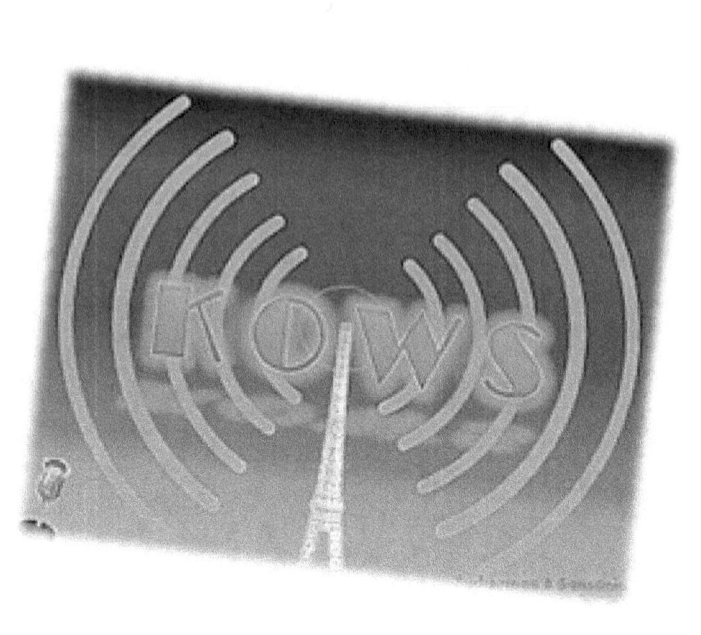

It is 1997. KOWS, a small Midwestern radio station, still broadcasts out of the same dusty studio where it began over 50 years ago. Time seems to have passed it by. KOWS is one of the last stations of its kind, where everything is still done live; old-style serials, music shows, newscasts, call-ins, etc. The station struggles to survive.

A musical comedy by Paul Zuckerman and Michael Sansonia.

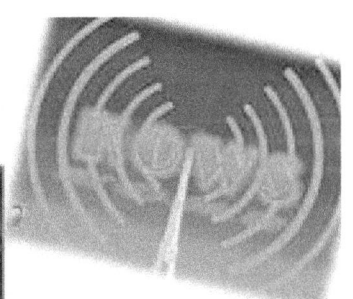

Act 1

1	"Public Enemies"
2	Next Day
3	Next Morning
4	"Unghar"
5	"Frontier Lawyer"
6	Next Day

Act 2

1	"Mysteries of History"
2	"Serials Marathon"
4	3 Days Later
5	Next Day

Dramatis Personnae

Jack Gatewood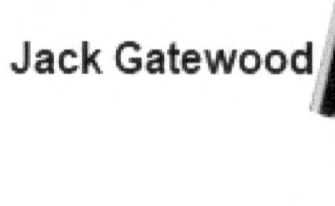

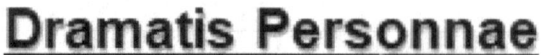 Al Gatewood

Eve Sommers

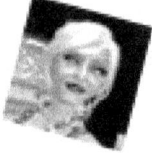 Desiree

Viss

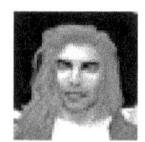 Foley

Denny Cadore

Wayne Barker

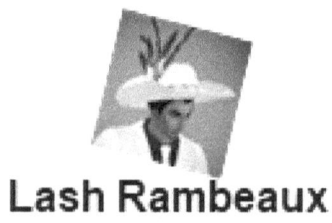 Lash Rambeaux

The Cast

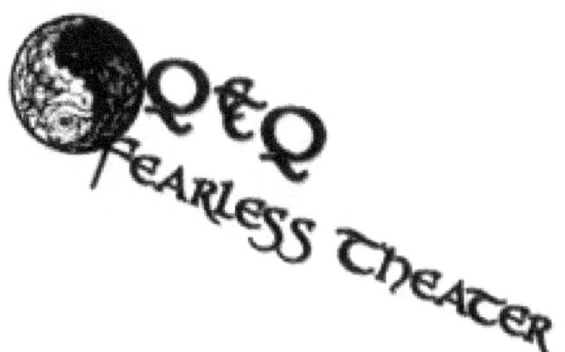

Q&Q
FEARLESS THEATER

KOWS

Jack		
	voice: Drew Scarlet	avatar: Sarah Elizabeth Brenham
Al		
	voice: Luhre Brann	avatar: Sarah Elizabeth Brenham
Eve		
	voice: Melita	avatar: Lady Thorn
Foley		
	voice: Action Jackson	avatar: Shy Corina
Desiree		
	voice: Lady Thorn	avatar: Melita
Denny		
	voice: Mist	avatar: Melita
Viss		
	voice: Jay Sparrowtree	avatar: Melita
Wayne Barker		
	voice: Action Jackson	avatar: Melita
Lash Rambeaux		
	voice: Luhre Brann	avatar: Melita

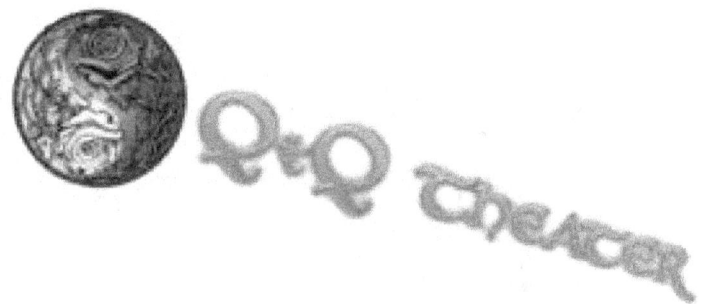

Creators

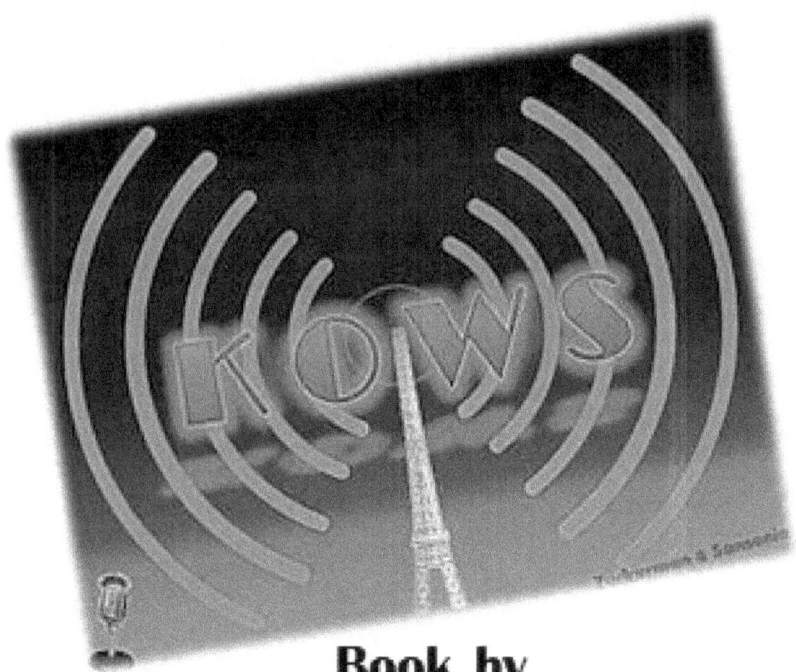

Book by
Paul Zuckerman
& Michael Sansonia

Music & Lyrics by
Michael Sansonia

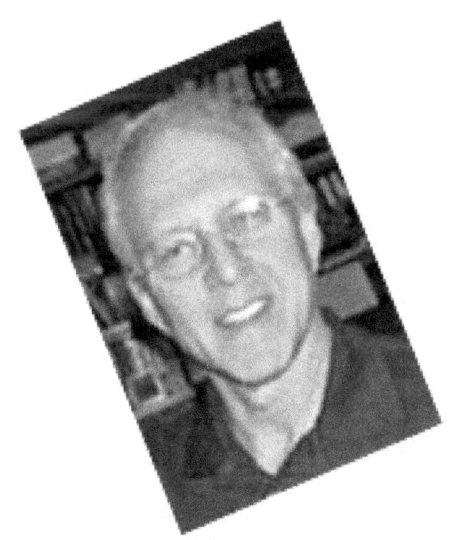

PAUL ZUCKERMAN (Director/Writer/Actor/Executive Producer) studied improvisation with Del Close and Jo Forsberg at The Second City in Chicago, and was an original cast member of Chicago City Limits. He helped bring the show to New York City, where he directed and performed with the company for over 10 years, and continues to direct and produce CCL comedy revues. Other directing credits include Comedy Et Al, television's first interactive comedy series, the Off-Broadway comedy Rosa Krantz and Gilda Stern Aren't Dead, and numerous shows for major corporations. He was anchorman for Chicago City Limits' TV series Reel News on the USA Network, appeared in the film Lovesick, TV's Cagney & Lacey, PBS's Reading Rainbow, Tales of the Unexpected and The Today Show. Paul also conducts idea generation sessions and focus groups for companies. He holds a doctoral degree in Psychology from the University of Michigan. Paul is married to Linda Gelman, with whom he co-produced Zara, Philip and Eli.

Michael Sansonia is a musical director, lyricist/composer, and music producer with an extremely varied background. He formed and performed with a Medieval ensemble for the premier of ROBIN AND MARIAN (starring Sean Connery), and a Country-Western band for the South African equivalent of the Kentucky Derby. He's a former musical director for National Lampoon's live shows and television specials, including CLASS OF '86, for which he also wrote several songs. Other television work includes the soundtrack PBS BIOGRAPHY, LIFESTYLES OF THE RICH AND FAMOUS, CNN TRAVEL SERIES, and the Jane Leeves sitcom THROB. During its original New York run, he conducted LITTLE SHOP OF HORRORS. He has appeared in several Broadway and off-Broadway shows as an actor/musician. These include PUMP BOYS AND DINETTES (he has, at one time or another, performed as each of the character/musicians in the onstage band) and SONG OF SINGAPORE. He has since musical directed several productions of PB&D. During the Toyota Comedy Festival, he was musical director and a contributing writer for FIRESIGN THEATRE. He has performed, arranged, or written music and lyrics for numerous corporate clients, such as MCI, Bayer, Nike, Verizon, Kraft Foods, Beneficial, Sandoz, Reliance, KPMG, CNN, Chase Manhattan, Scholastic, Hallmark, and many others.

TWILIGHT ZONE

An Afternoon in the Twilight Zone

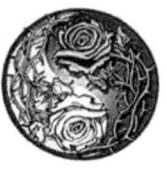

Q&Q FEARLESS Theater

The Twilight Zone is an American television anthology series created by Rod Serling. The episodes are in various genres, including psychological horror, fantasy, science fiction, suspense, and psychological thriller; and often conclude with a macabre or unexpected twist, and usually with a moral. A popular and critical success, it introduced many Americans to common science fiction and fantasy tropes. The original series, shot entirely in black and white, ran for five seasons from 1959 to 1964.

Episodes

The Lonely

A World of His Own

The Lonely   [Rod Serling]

In 2046, an inmate named Corry is sentenced to solitary confinement on a distant asteroid for 50 years. In his fourth year of confinement, he is visited by a spacecraft (commanded by a Captain Allenby) that brings him supplies and news from the Earth four times a year. The ship and crew can stay for only a few minutes each visit, as the asteroid's orbit and the ship's fuel consumption rate make longer visits impossible, lest the space-traveling delivery crew would be stuck for 2 weeks or more, awaiting favorable orbit conditions to depart..

Dramatis Personnae

Corry

Allenby

Adams

Carstairs

Alicia

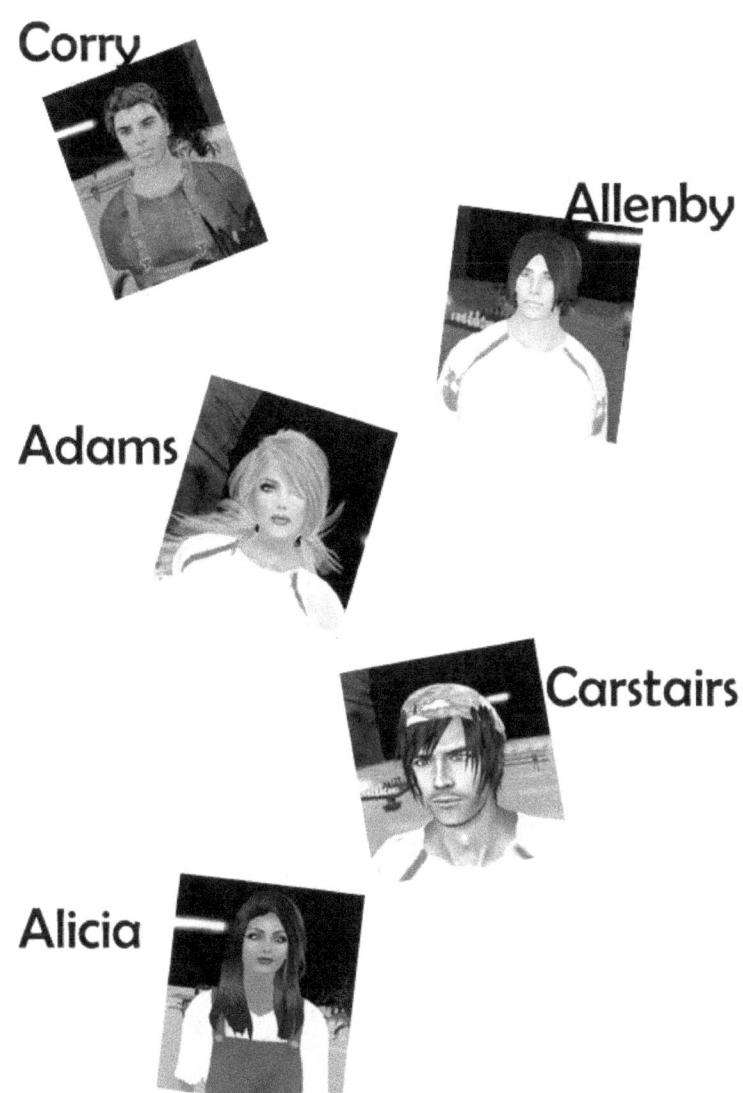

World of His Own [Richard Matheson]

Coming home, Victoria West spots her husband, playwright Gregory West, through the window sharing a drink in his study with Mary, an attractive, affectionate blonde. When Victoria barges into the room, Mary is nowhere to be found.

Gregory explains to his wife that any character that he describes into his dictation machine will appear according to his description. To make the character disappear, all he has to do is cut out that portion of the tape and throw it into his fireplace.

Dramatis Personnae

Gregory West

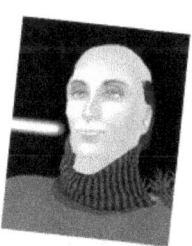

Mary

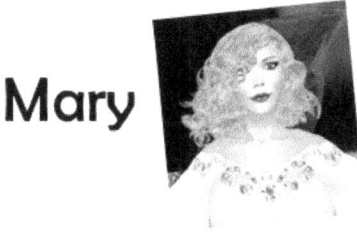

Victoria West

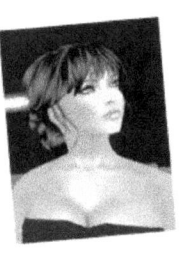

The Cast

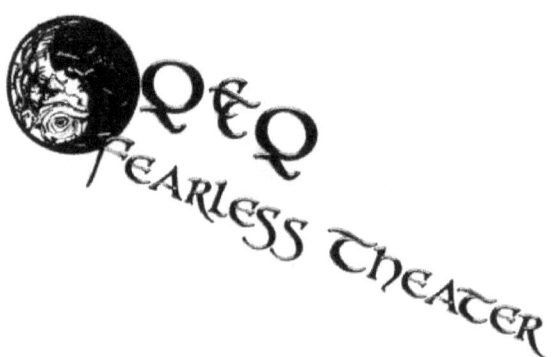

QEQ
FEARLESS THEATER

THE LONELY

Corry		
	voice: Action Jackson	avateer: Sarah Elizabeth Brenham
Allenby		
	voice: Jay Sparrowtree	avateer: Drew Scarlet
Adams		
	voice: Mist	avateer: Lady Thorn
Alicia		
	voice: Lady Thorn	avateer: Shy Corina
Carstairs		
		avateer: Melita

A WORLD OF HIS OWN

Gregory West		
	voice: Luhre Brann	avateer: Sarah Elizabeth Brenham
Mary		
	voice: Melita	avateer: Drew Scarlet
Victoria West		
	voice: Shy Corina	avateer: Action Jackson

PYGMALION

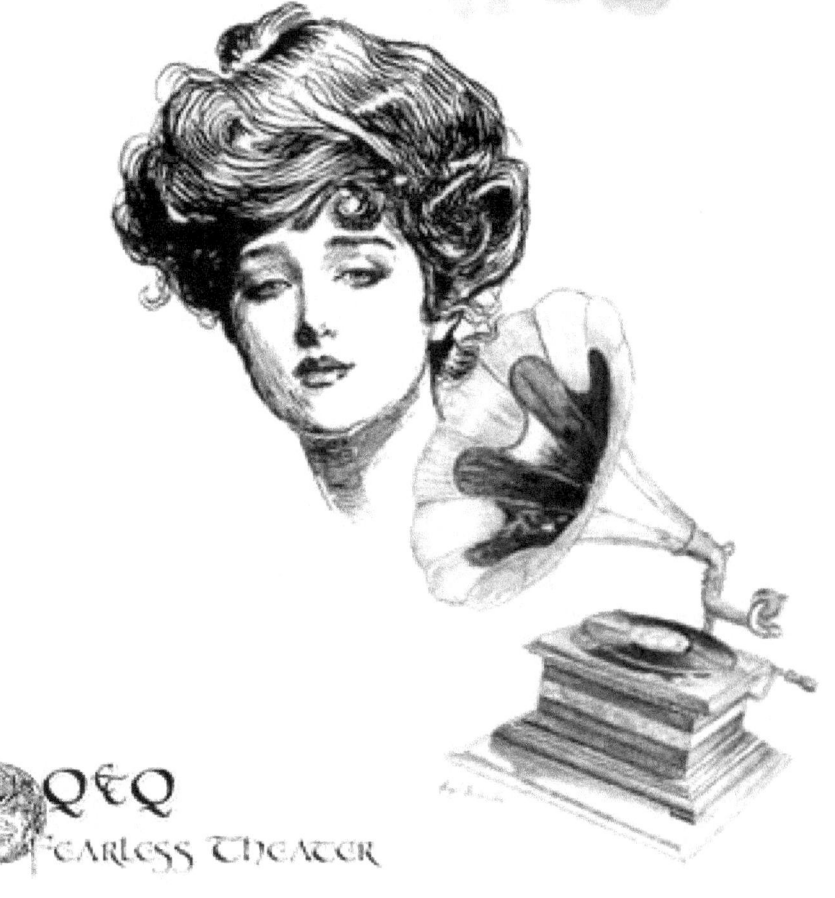

George Bernard Shaw's
Pygmalion

Q&Q
FEARLESS THEATER

Pygmalion

is a play by George Bernard Shaw, named after a Greek mythological figure. It was first presented to the public on stage in 1913.

In ancient Greek mythology, Pygmalion fell in love with one of his sculptures, which then came to life. The general idea of that myth was a popular subject for Victorian era English playwrights. Shaw's play has been adapted numerous times, most notably as the musical My Fair Lady and its film version.

Highlights—
Programme

Act II – Wimpole Street

Act V – Mrs. Higgins' Conservatory

Dramatis Personnae

Henry Higgins

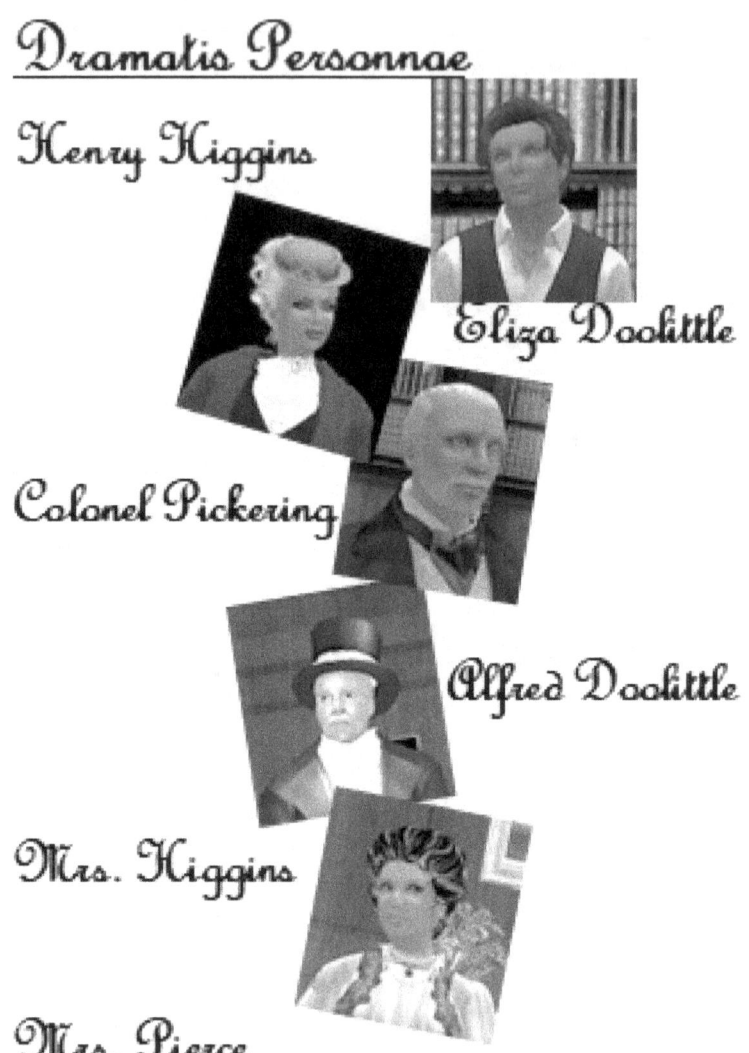

Eliza Doolittle

Colonel Pickering

Alfred Doolittle

Mrs. Higgins

Mrs. Pierce

Parlor Maid

The Cast

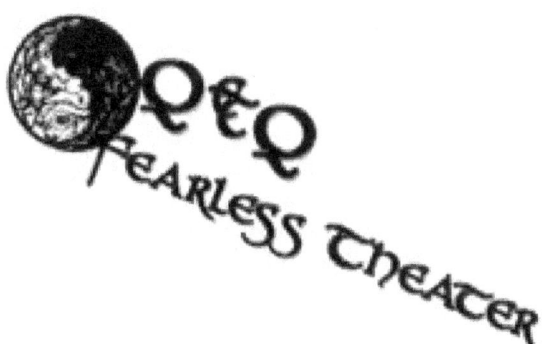

Q&Q
FEARLESS THEATER

Pygmalion

Henry Higgins		
	twins: Luhre Brann	*nice twins:* Sarah Elizabeth Branham
Eliza Doolittle		
	twins: Melita	*nice twins:* Shy Corina
Colonel Pickering		
	twins: Jawahir	*nice twins:* Mist
Mrs Higgins		
	twins: Lady Thorn	*nice twins:* Drex Scarlet
Alfred Doolittle		
	twins: Action Jackson	*nice twins:* Lady Thorn
Mrs Pierced		
	twins: Mist	*nice twins:* Drex Scarlet
Parlor Maid		
	twins: Lady Thorn	*nice twins:* Melita

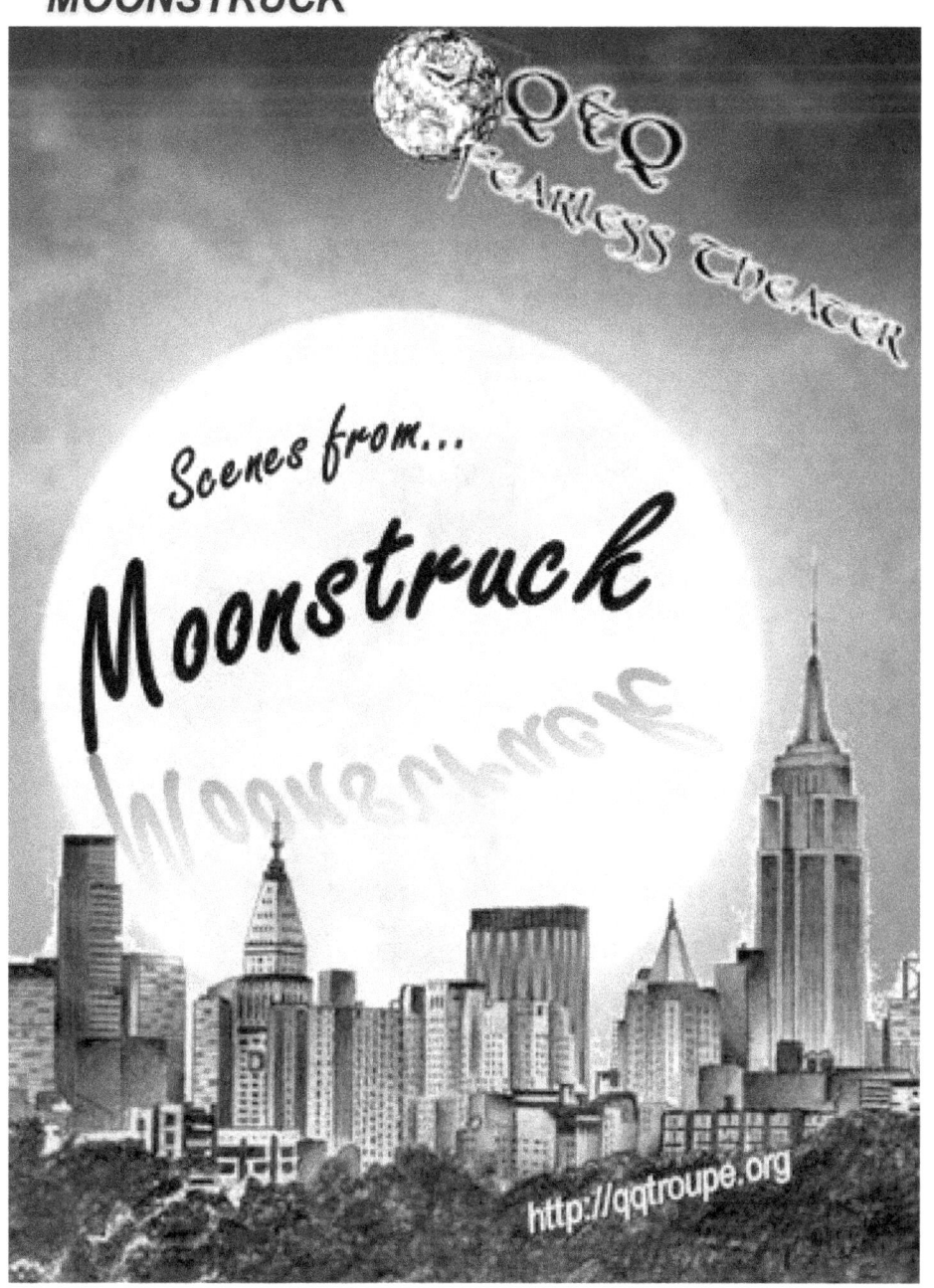

MOONSTRUCK [John Patrick Shanley]

That most charming Academy Award winning movie...

No sooner does Italian-American widow Loretta accept a marriage proposal from her doltish boyfriend, Johnny, than she finds herself falling for his younger brother, Ronny. She tries to resist, but Ronny has no scruples about aggressively pursuing her while Johnny is out of the country. As Loretta falls deeper in love, everything changes.

Rotten Tomatoes review says:
"Moonstruck is an exuberantly funny tribute to love and one of the decade's most appealing comedies"

Scenes

Thursday

- Work Day
- Evening

Friday

- Morning
- Dinner
- That CRAZY Moon

Saturday

- Morning

Dramatis Personnae

Loretta Castorini

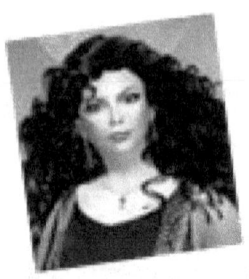

RonnyCammareri

JohnnyCammareri

Cosmo Castorini

Rose Castorini

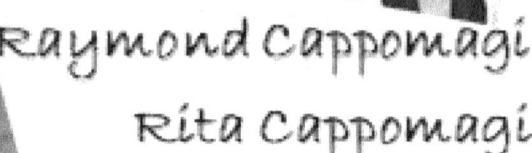

Raymond Cappomagi

Rita Cappomagi

Old Mr. Castorini

Irv
Lotti

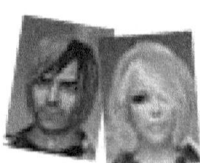

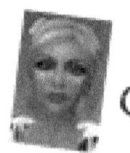

Chrissy

The Cast

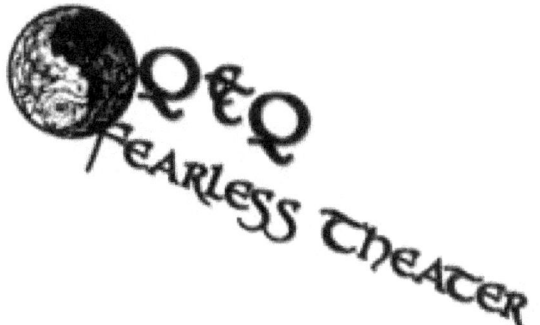

Moonstruck

	voice:	actor:
Loretta Castorini	Lahro Braxx	Sarah Elizabeth Brenham
Rose Castorini	Melita	Shy Corina
Cosmo Castorini	Jawahir	Mist
Old Dad Castorini	Lady Thorn	Drew Scarlet
Raymond Cappomaggi	Action Jackson	Lady Thorn
Rita Cappomaggi	Mist	Drew Scarlet

Roxxy Camereri		
	wife: Action Jackson	unborn: Sarah Elizabeth Branham
Johnny Camereri		
	wife: Jawahir	unborn: Shy Corina
Zito		
	wife: Fritz Gregory	
Conti		
	wife: LaKrce Brown	
Florit		
	wife: Jawahir	
Mook		
	wife: LaKrce Brown	
Iro		
	wife: Ron Phoenix	
Lott		
	wife: Rose Artffax	

KOWS

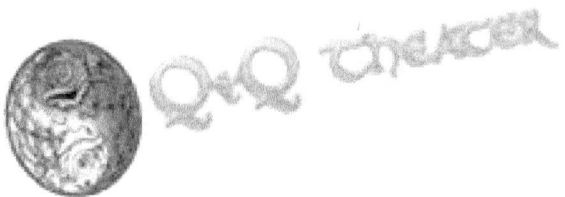

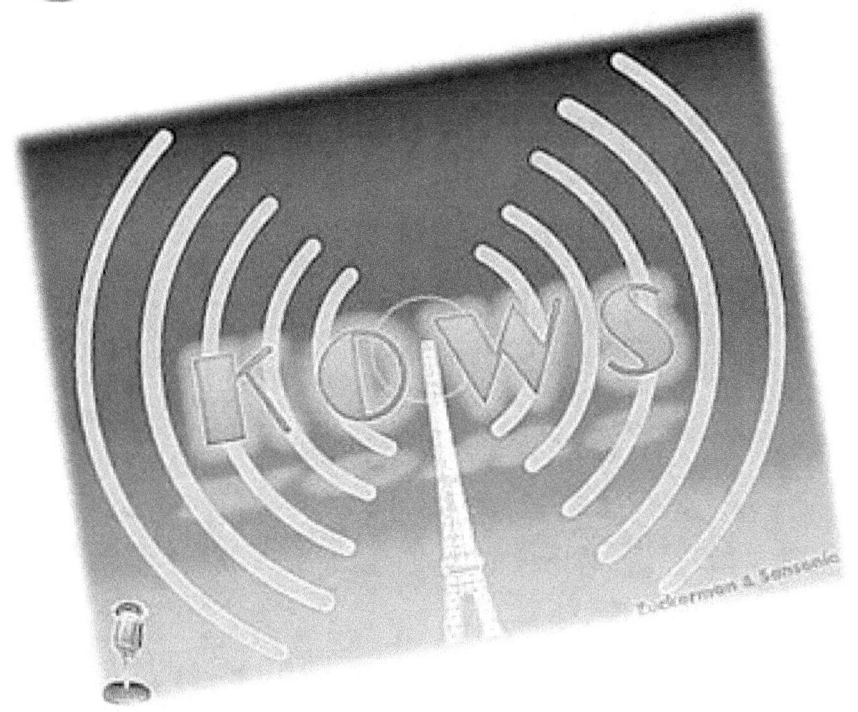

At

http://qqtroupe.org

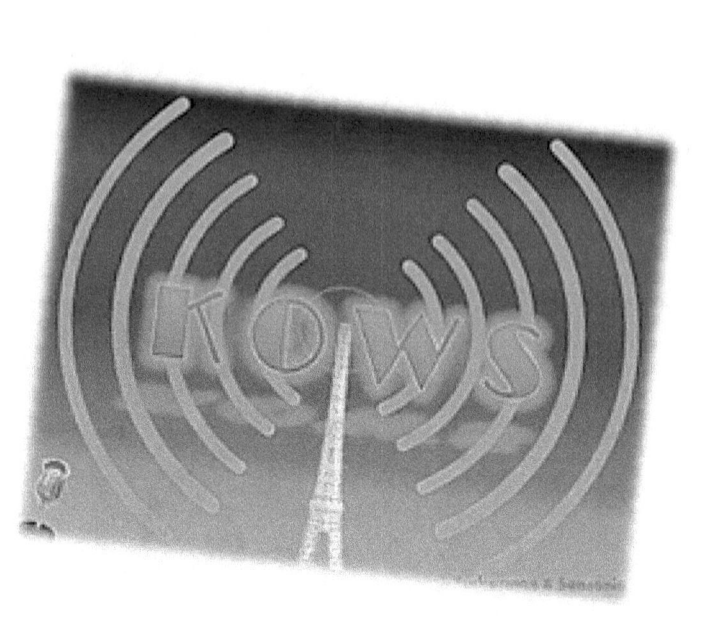

It is 1997. KOWS, a small Midwestern radio station, still broadcasts out of the same dusty studio where it began over 50 years ago. Time seems to have passed it by. KOWS is one of the last stations of its kind, where everything is still done live; old-style serials, music shows, newscasts, call-ins, etc. The station struggles to survive.

A musical comedy by Paul Zuckerman and Michael Sansonia.

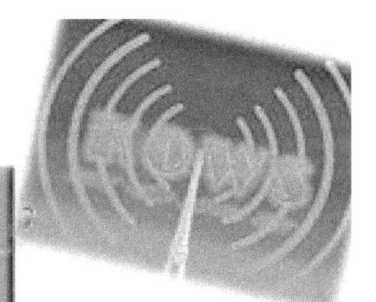

Act 1

1	"Public Enemies"
2	Next Day
3	Next Morning
4	"Unghar"
5	"Frontier Lawyer"
6	Next Day

Act 2

1	"Mysteries of History"
2	"Serials Marathon"
4	3 Days Later
5	Next Day

Dramatis Personnae

Jack Gatewood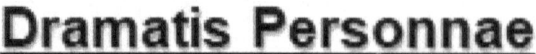

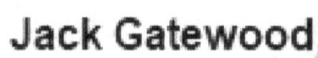 Al Gatewood

Eve Sommers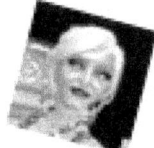

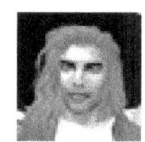 Desiree

Viss

Foley

Denny Cadore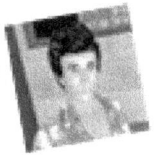

Wayne Barker

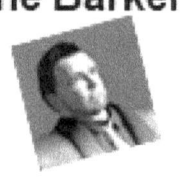

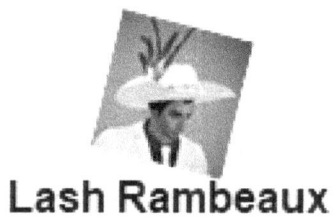

Lash Rambeaux

The Cast

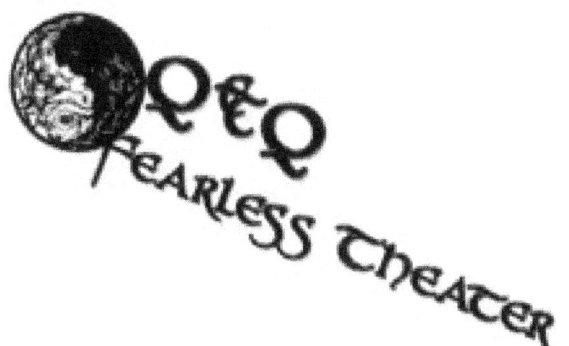

Q&Q
FEARLESS THEATER

KOWS

	voice	avatar
Jack		
	Drew Scarlet	Sarah Elizabeth Brenham
Al		
	Luhre Brann	Sarah Elizabeth Brenham
Eve		
	Melita	Lady Thorn
Foley		
	Action Jackson	Shy Corina
Desiree		
	Lady Thorn	Melita
Denny		
	Mist	Melita
Viss		
	Jay Sparrowtree	Melita
Wayne Barker		
	Action Jackson	Melita
Lash Rambeaux		
	Luhre Brann	Melita

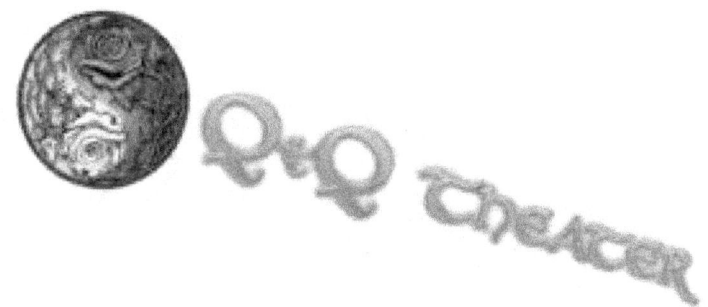

Creators

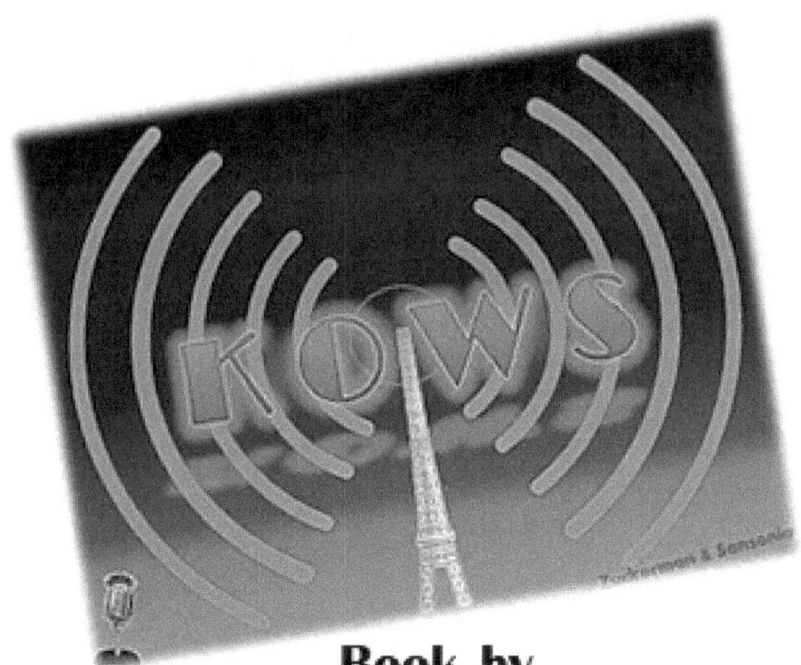

**Book by
Paul Zuckerman
& Michael Sansonia**

**Music & Lyrics by
Michael Sansonia**

http://qqtroupe.wix.com/kows

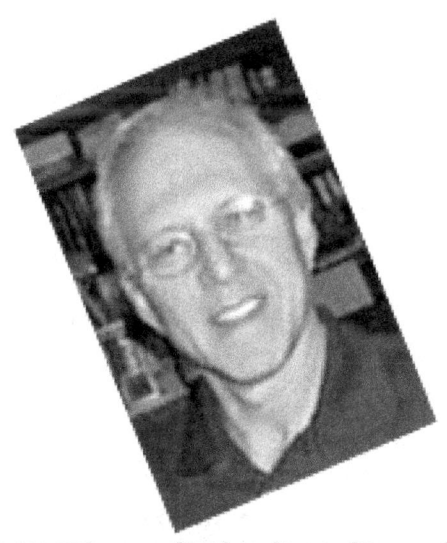

PAUL ZUCKERMAN (Director/Writer/Actor/Executive Producer) studied improvisation with Del Close and Jo Forsberg at The Second City in Chicago, and was an original cast member of Chicago City Limits. He helped bring the show to New York City, where he directed and performed with the company for over 10 years, and continues to direct and produce CCL comedy revues. Other directing credits include Comedy Et Al, television's first interactive comedy series, the Off-Broadway comedy Rosa Krantz and Gilda Stern Aren't Dead, and numerous shows for major corporations. He was anchorman for Chicago City Limits' TV series Reel News on the USA Network, appeared in the film Lovesick, TV's Cagney & Lacey, PBS's Reading Rainbow, Tales of the Unexpected and The Today Show. Paul also conducts idea generation sessions and focus groups for companies. He holds a doctoral degree in Psychology from the University of Michigan. Paul is married to Linda Gelman, with whom he co-produced Zara, Philip and Eli.

Michael Sansonia is a musical director, lyricist/composer, and music producer with an extremely varied background. He formed and performed with a Medieval ensemble for the premier of ROBIN AND MARIAN (starring Sean Connery), and a Country-Western band for the South African equivalent of the Kentucky Derby. He's a former musical director for National Lampoon's live shows and television specials, including CLASS OF '86, for which he also wrote several songs. Other television work includes the soundtrack PBS BIOGRAPHY, LIFESTYLES OF THE RICH AND FAMOUS, CNN TRAVEL SERIES, and the Jane Leeves sitcom THROB. During its original New York run, he conducted LITTLE SHOP OF HORRORS. He has appeared in several Broadway and off-Broadway shows as an actor/musician. These include PUMP BOYS AND DINETTES (he has, at one time or another, performed as each of the character/musicians in the onstage band) and SONG OF SINGAPORE. He has since musical directed several productions of PB&D. During the Toyota Comedy Festival, he was musical director and a contributing writer for FIRESIGN THEATRE. He has performed, arranged, or written music and lyrics for numerous corporate clients, such as MCI, Bayer, Nike, Verizon, Kraft Foods, Beneficial, Sandoz, Reliance, KPMG, CNN, Chase Manhattan, Scholastic, Hallmark, and many others.

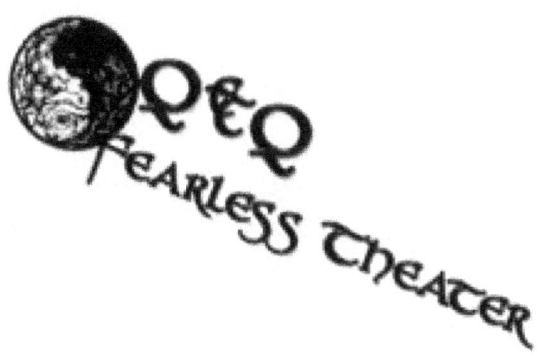

The
Company

ABOUT JO KARABASZ 'KAR-A-BASS'

[Rose Artifex online]

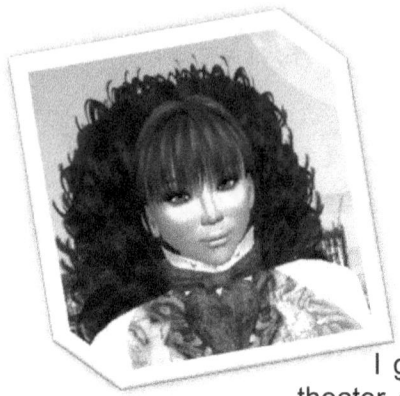

I've been an actor since elementary school and a radio broadcaster for nearly three decades. I had a vision of theater in a virtual world, and am blessed with very smart friends who all seem prepared to attempt the impossible.

I grew up with a Dad who loved all things theater and a Mom who loved books. I took a minor in Shakespeare even while I studied at the Wharton School of Business, and have acted and directed as a teacher every chance I got ever since.

I am a teacher, a published writer, a tech geek, and a person blessed – or cursed – with a restless mind.

I began my online life in the 1990's in text-based chat rooms. In that realm I was a busy radio broadcaster, and I made more than a few attempts to present theatrical entertainment. We did radio drama to appreciative audiences, but 'way' back then broadcasting as a group was well-nigh impossible. Theatricals in text without any acting or visuals – well, they just weren't good enough.

THEN! I heard about Second Life. In November of 2010 I stepped into this virtual world and have not looked back since; I came exploring with the sole purpose of turning it toward theatrical entertainment. I've spent every extra hour since then doing so.

The Quill & Quarrel Theater had its first rehearsal on July 15th, 2011.

Had you ever before that time asked me how I planned to change the world, 'creating a theatrical art form' would not have appeared on that list anywhere, but this experience of envisioning new possibilities then forcing them into existence has been like nothing else in my life: heady and wonderful! I am more lucky than I can say to have such smart, talented friends to do it with.

I renamed us the *Q&Q FEARLESS Theater* in 2016 to give honor to these amazing people. For each production we do, I target a few areas in which we will push forward into uncharted territory. I say, "OK, let's do these ridiculous, impossible things nobody has ever tried before!" and a dozen people answer, "OK, let's do THAT!" and promptly figure out how to make them happen. What more could I ever want?

THE FEARLESS ONES

The Q&Q is more inclusive than any traditional theater could ever be. Both our members and our audience are located all over the globe. The Internet makes time zones and distance irrelevant, but even more significant is the fact that disability or age is no obstacle: several of our cast members are seriously hampered either in terms of mobility or vision – and one cannot speak – but they can and do act in our productions. In the same way, we can bring theater to those who are homebound or simply live too far from a city to have live theater available to them.

The troupe has all the same functions any company has: Director, Actor, Costumer, Designer, Tech Crew. And then MORE.

Here are some of the animation-specific tasks, things that you wouldn't expect if you are a Broadway theater aficionado.

First, we have voice actors like any animated production does. They are working from ONLY what they hear. It isn't possible to watch the stage action because of technical considerations and even worse – they can't see each other because the company is spread all across the world. The INTERNET makes it possible for us to work together.

Second, we have Avateers. What is an Avateer? This is the actor who moves the avatar on stage. This means listening to the sound the audience hears and synchronizing action and even moving the lips of the avatar. These are the detailed technologists of the production

What sort of programming needs to be done? Well, there's the stage manager's display, which allows them to start various special effects, like curtains going up or down, explosions, rockets, even set changes. Someone has to make the stage manager's display (called a HUD - a Head's Up Display) do all its magic, and that is one of the programmer's roles. And then there are the magical effects: where writing appears on a blackboard, fog drifts across the audience, snow falls from the sky. It's more programming of a particular type, called 'particle magic'. These are all specialties of our master programmer!

Last but not least, is the choreographer. Well, choreographer is straight forward, right? You just tell the dancers what to do? Nope. An avatar, by itself, will just stand there. With an Avateer at the helm, it will walk or run. But you can't make it dance. Fortunately, there are a great many very talented animators working in Second Life who create dance animations we can use in our productions. Then, you start the animation. But if you wait for the avateers to start the dances, they will all be happening at slightly different times. The choreographer not only chooses the dances but also makes the tools that allow all of the animations start at the same time.

Complicated? You bet! These people step out over and over to make our magic happen.

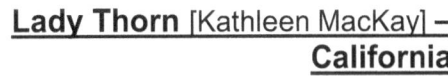

Lady Thorn [Kathleen MacKay] – **California**

She is a singer, actress, and rose-lover. She has been active in classical-based (primarily Shakespearean) community theatre for over a decade, and has been performing at historical reenactment events for over 20 years. Currently, Kathleen is the Director of Dotter's Knot, a women's a cappella vocal group. When not on stage, she can be found singing to her roses.

Kathleen's role within the Q and Q is not limited to voice acting and avateering. She has become the Mistress of the Costumes: coordinating, crafting, and "dressing" each avatar with a pain-staking and often obsessive compulsive commitment to the over-all look of each production.

Action Jackson [Ken Raney] - **Texas**

A lifelong fan of film and theater, Ken became involved in high school theater and carried that through into college, where he majored in Art. After many years of non-involvement, he encountered Texas Radio Theater Company, where, for the past 15 years, he and the group have performed in the fashion of Old Time Radio before live audiences, doing old radio programs and original stories. While with TRTC he has performed as announcer, live sound effects man, and in various acting roles. Many of TRTC's shows are currently available online as podcasts.

Since entering Second Life, Ken has produced, directed, and acted in a number of plays. Currently he acts in the Q&Q and ACT theater groups.

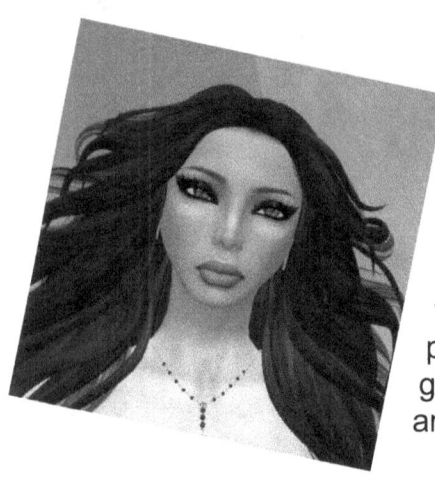

Sarah Brenham - New Jersey

Sarah has been a citizen of Second Life for over ten years. She has been our MASTER AVATEER for 7 of those years. In this realm, she enjoys working, role-playing, and dancing. When she's not in SL, she can be found reading, shopping, and watching TV programs. Sarah's personality can best be described as giving, authentic, empathetic, honest, and quiet.

Luhre Brann [Larry Brown] - California

Larry is a retired college instructor of Chemistry and a standardized test preparation tutor in the real world. His entertainment experience before the Q&Q was almost entirely as a musician – classical and rock. As a result of his long acquaintance with its creator, at the inception of the Q&Q he was dragged "kicking and screaming" into the project. He has been a part of every production since the beginning and, don't tell the boss, but he says he'd never quit now.

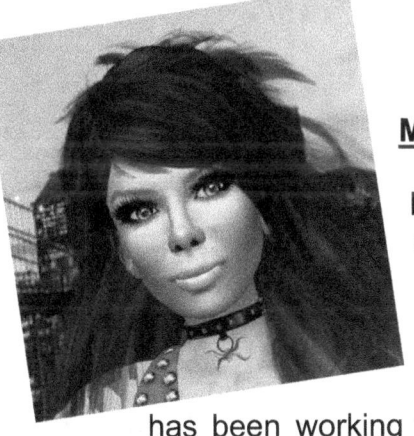

Melita [Sue Schroeder] - Maryland

Tech Crew (stage hand, set building, costuming) in college. Her real life job is script writing for training videos. She is an aspiring novelist and an unpaid novel editor.

More germane to her work here, she has been working with the Quill and Quarrel Fearless Theater Second Life since 2015.

Her acting credits include
Blithe Spirit: Elvira.
MidSummer Night's Dream: Puck.
Pygmallion: Eliza Doolittle.
Twilight Zone/The Lonely: crew member.
Twilight Zone/A world of his Own: Mary.
Twilight Zone/Seven characters without an exit: Ballerina.
Moonstruck: Rose, Chrissy.

Technical credits include:
Wit, Blithe Spirit, Midsummer Night's Dream, KOWS, Pygmallion, Twilight Zone, Moonstruck.

In the best traditions of community theater, Sue has worn many technical hats as well. She has faithfully performed (with hardly any complaining!) the technical roles of: Simulcast closed captioning, avateer, programmer, various magical effects, choreographer, set and prop construction, costuming, photographer, advertising, assistant director, and stage manager!

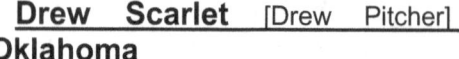

Drew Scarlet [Drew Pitcher] - Oklahoma

New to the Q&Q, Drew did some local offline Community Theater and performed in plays while in the military. Titles he has appeared in include: "Not with My Daughter", "South Pacific", "The Night Is My Enemy", and "The Mouse that Roared".

Shy Corina [Carol Williams] – Texas

Carol grew up dancing ballet and acting in grade school and high school play productions. She acts with the Q&Q, as well as with "ACT", in Second Life. She also danced for Ballet Pixelle for a number of years, during which she worked on several solo performances.

Dancing is her passion, along with acting with her SL Partner, Action Jackson86. She has choreographed several dance numbers for "White Christmas" and the musical "Grease".

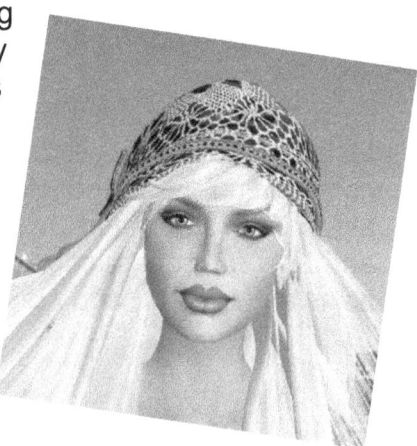

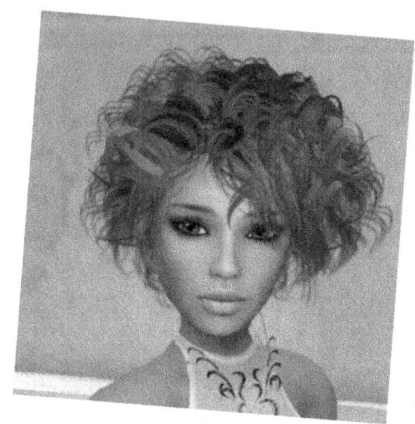

Mist [Julie Woodbury] - Minnesota

Julie is a recovering academic. She dabbled in theatre for several decades from elementary school through her early thirties, after which she taught communication courses, including public speaking, for two decades.She has often been accused of being a character; she is capitalizing upon that attribute with the Q&Q.

Jay Sparrowtree [Jim Bowen] - Tennessee

Jim has been part of the Q&Q for about 5 years now. He first got hooked on acting at a young age with grade school and high school drama and choral groups. Later, at a local church, he performed in several on-stage productions. His work in these included running the sound and multimedia systems. He now owns and operates a popular Internet Radio Station, which may be found at http://worldwidewhip.com.

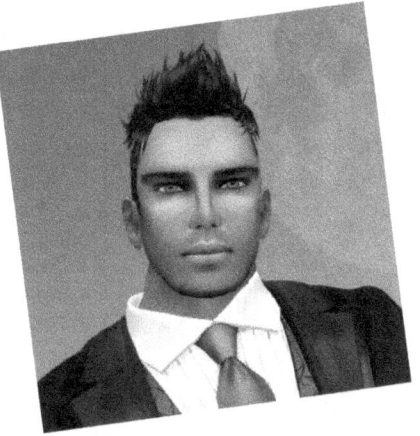

Marcus Galbreus [Corey Shelsta] – **Designer and Professor of Theatre at South Dakota State University.**

Corey designs lighting, scenery, and sound for productions at SDSU as well as other theatres in the region. Additionally, he teaches courses in design, technical production, and theatre history. His interests include incorporating digital technology and virtual reality simulations into the classroom and the stage. During the summer Corey is the production manager for Prairie Repertory Theatre. Before coming to SDSU, Corey was the resident lighting and sound designer at Theatre Memphis in Memphis, TN. Corey's awards include SDSU Artist of the Year for "An Evening with Harvey Dunn's Feminine Images"; Broadway World Sioux Falls Region Award for "Shrek: the Musical" (Lighting Design) and "Hairspray" (Lighting Design); Detroit Free Press Theatre award for "Beyond the Horizon" (Lighting Design), and Memphis Theatre Awards for "Joseph and the Amazing Technicolor Dreamcoat" (Lighting Design), "As Bees in Honey Drown" (Original Music), "Gypsy" (Sound Design), and "A Piece of My Heart" (Sound Design). Recent designs include scenic and projection design for "A Christmas Carol" and lighting design for "True West" and "Six Characters in Search of an Author" at South Dakota State University; lighting design for "The Wizard of Oz" at Minnesota State University, Moorehead; scenic design for "Sister Act" and lighting and scenic design for "The Full Monty" at Prairie Repertory Theatre. Last summer, he directed "I Love You, You're Perfect, Now Change" for Prairie Repertory Theatre. Corey is active in the Northern Boundary Section of USITT, and serves as regional chair. Corey and his wife Stacy have two children, Preston and Ainsley, both of whom have been coming to the theatre since before they were old enough to walk. When he is not teaching, designing or mentoring student designers, he can be found getting his fingers tangled up in guitar and banjo strings, mowing his lawn, or running model trains around his basement.

> "HUMANS HAD BUILT A WORLD INSIDE THE WORLD,
> WHICH REFLECTED IT IN PRETTY MUCH THE SAME WAY
> AS A DROP OF WATER REFLECTED THE LANDSCAPE. AND
> YET ... AND YET ...
>
> TERRY PRATCHETT, WYRD SISTERS

THE WORLD OF SECOND LIFE

Second Life is an online virtual world, developed and owned by the San Francisco-based firm Linden Lab and launched on June 23, 2003. By 2013, Second Life had approximately one million regular users. Now in 2018 at any time of the day or night there are 30,000 or more people in Second Life pursuing a dazzling variety of activities.

In many ways, Second Life is similar to massively multiplayer online role-playing games; however, Linden Lab is emphatic that their creation is *not* a game: "There is no manufactured conflict, no set objective". Indeed, Second Life is whatever the users of the platform build it to be.

Second Life users create virtual representations of themselves, called avatars, and are able to interact with places, objects, and other avatars. They can explore the world, meet other residents, socialize, participate in both individual and group activities, build, create, shop, and trade virtual property and services with one another.

The platform principally features 3D-based user-generated content. Built into the software is a 3D modeling tool based on simple geometric shapes that allows residents to build virtual objects. There is also a procedural scripting language, Linden Scripting Language, which can be used to add interactivity to objects.

In this virtual world we build our theater, construct our sets, hold our rehearsals, and create cinema-like visual effects.

Without a doubt there are limitations in animation as compared to physical performance – but, OH! There are also huge advantages! We can 'do' what would never be possible in a physical theater – and, eventually, almost anything that moviemakers can do, we will be able to do LIVE.

PRODUCTION HISTORY

Since 2011 the Q&Q has produced 2 or 3 shows a year. We tour the Second Life world and perform to more than 1000 people each year.

Many of our early shows were fan fiction we wrote ourselves, but in 2013 we were finally ready to undertake something more ambitious. We produced Margaret Edson's "Wit" and convinced ourselves, at least, that 'real' theater was possible in our virtual world.

As our technology and skills have improved, our range has broadened until we can look back and say we have presented: [* - home movies of the show can be found on YouTube or our web site]

- 2013 - "The Happy Prince"
- 2013 - "Wit"*
- 2013 - "All in the Timing"
- 2015 - "A Midsummer Night's Dream"
- 2015 - "Almost Maine"*
- 2016 - "KOWS"* - never been produced except by the Q&Q
- 2016 - "Blithe Spirit"*
- 2017 - "Moonstruck"
- 2017 - "Twilight Zone"*
- 2018 - "Pygmalion"

Scrapbook

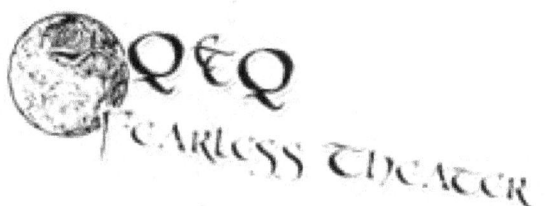

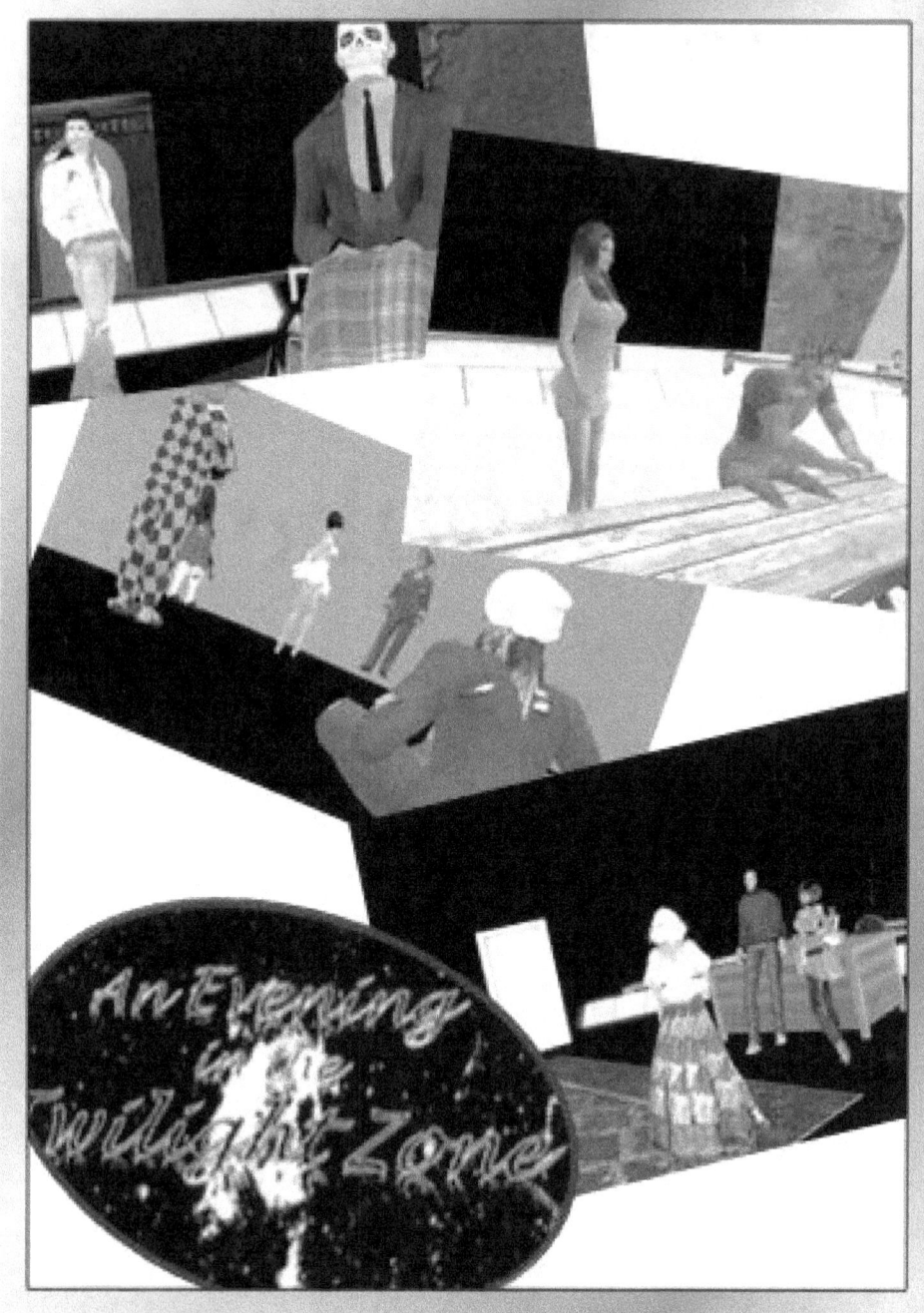

An Evening in the Twilight Zone

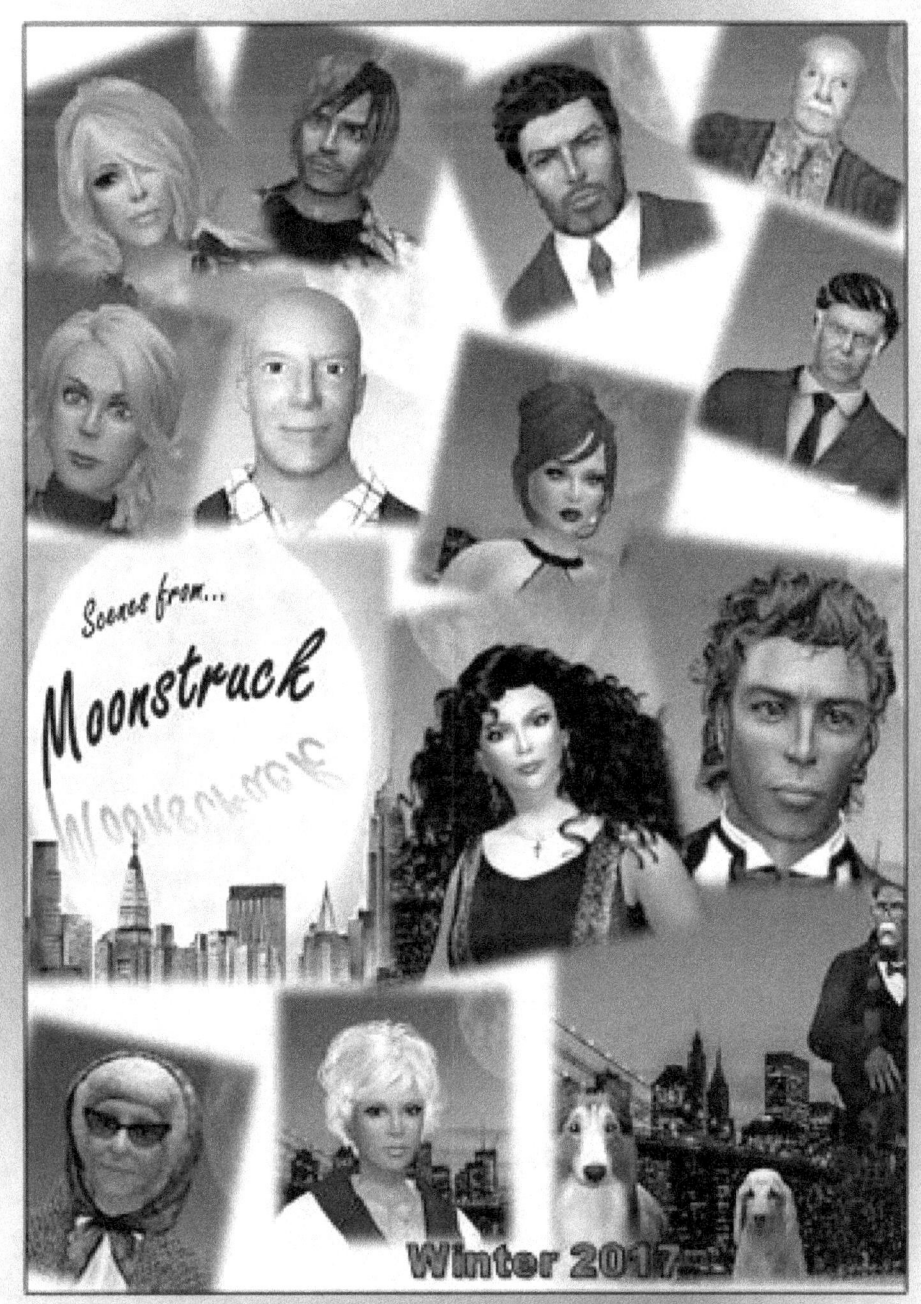

Scenes from...

Moonstruck

Winter 2017

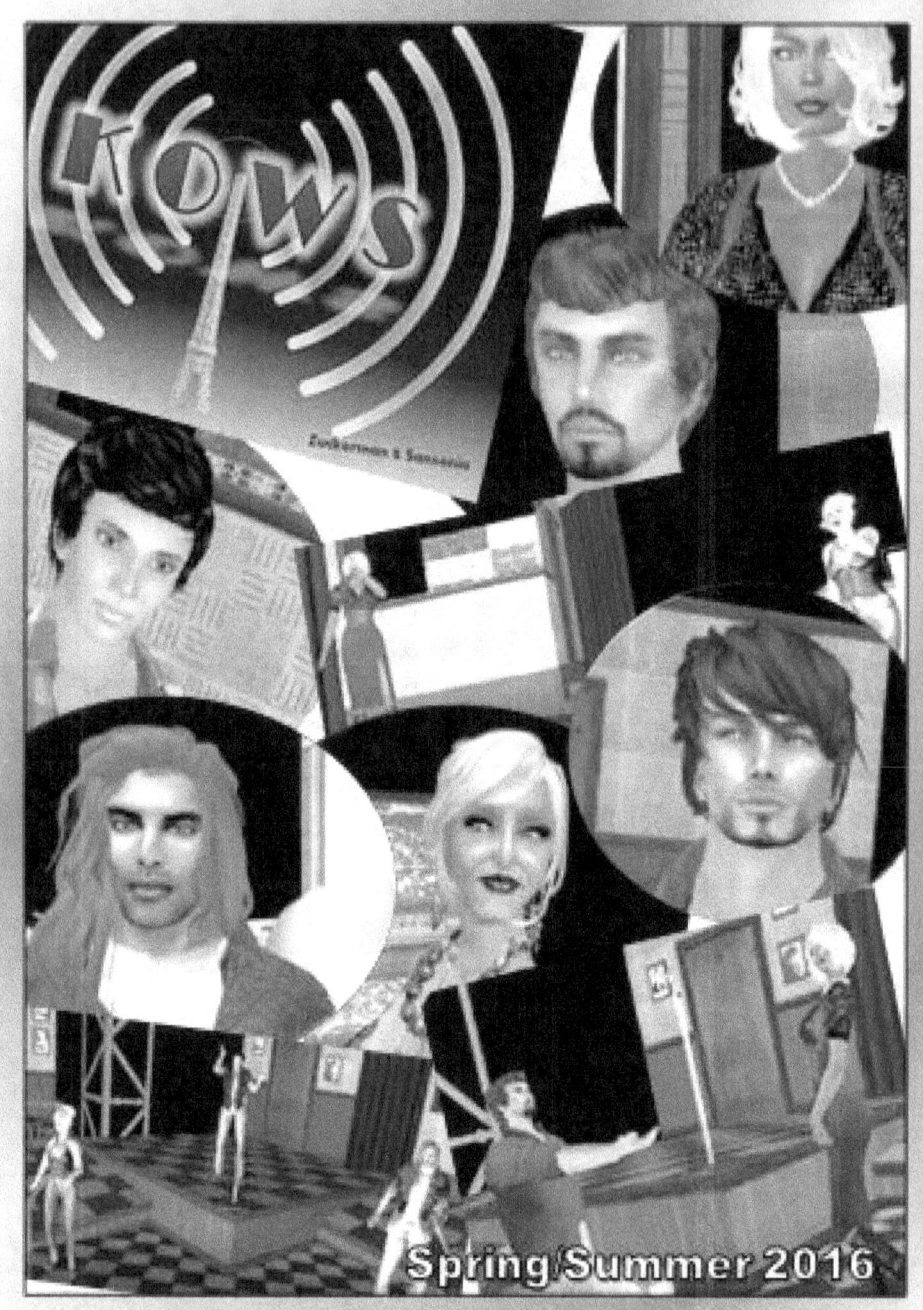

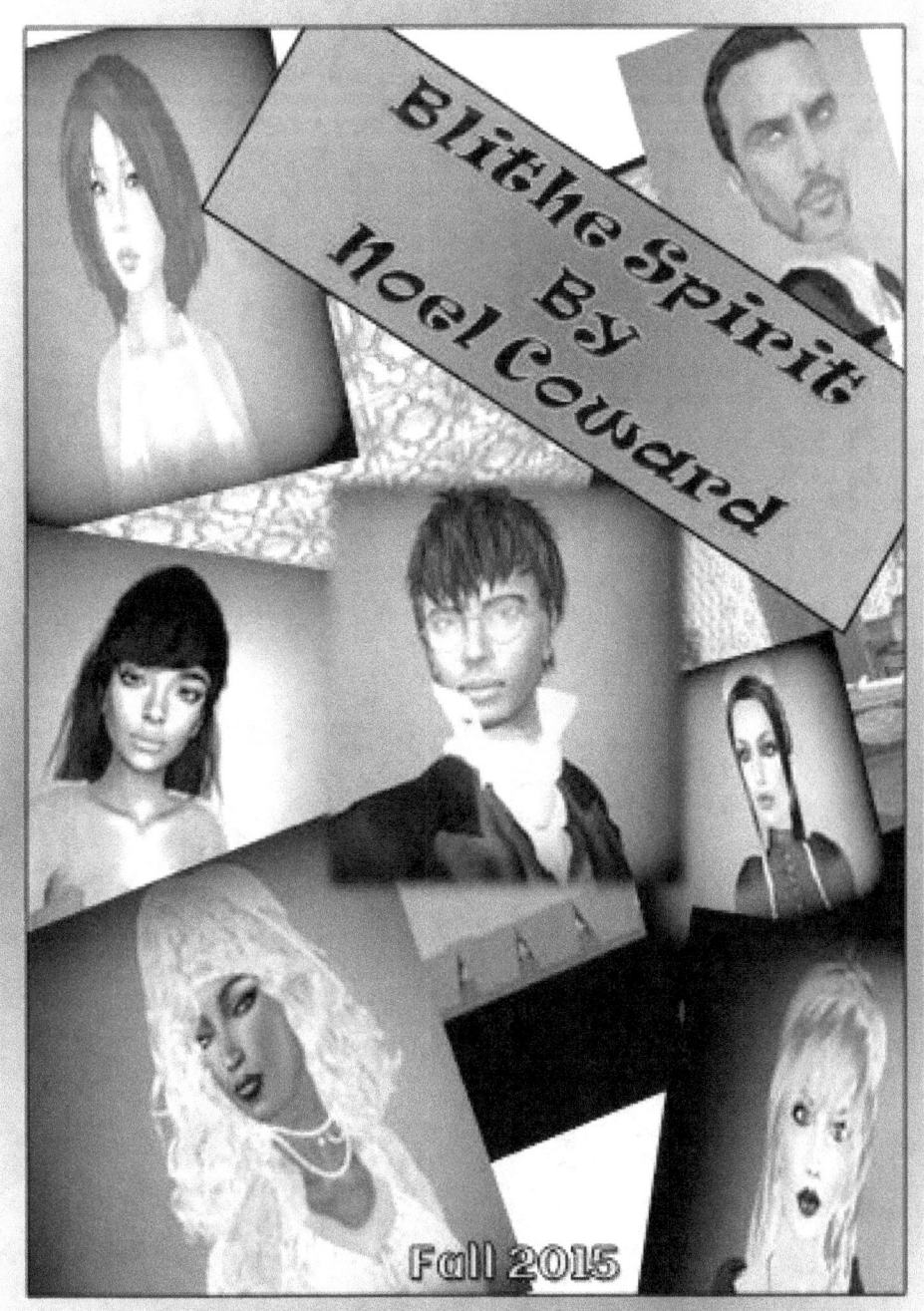

Blithe Spirit By Noel Coward

Fall 2015

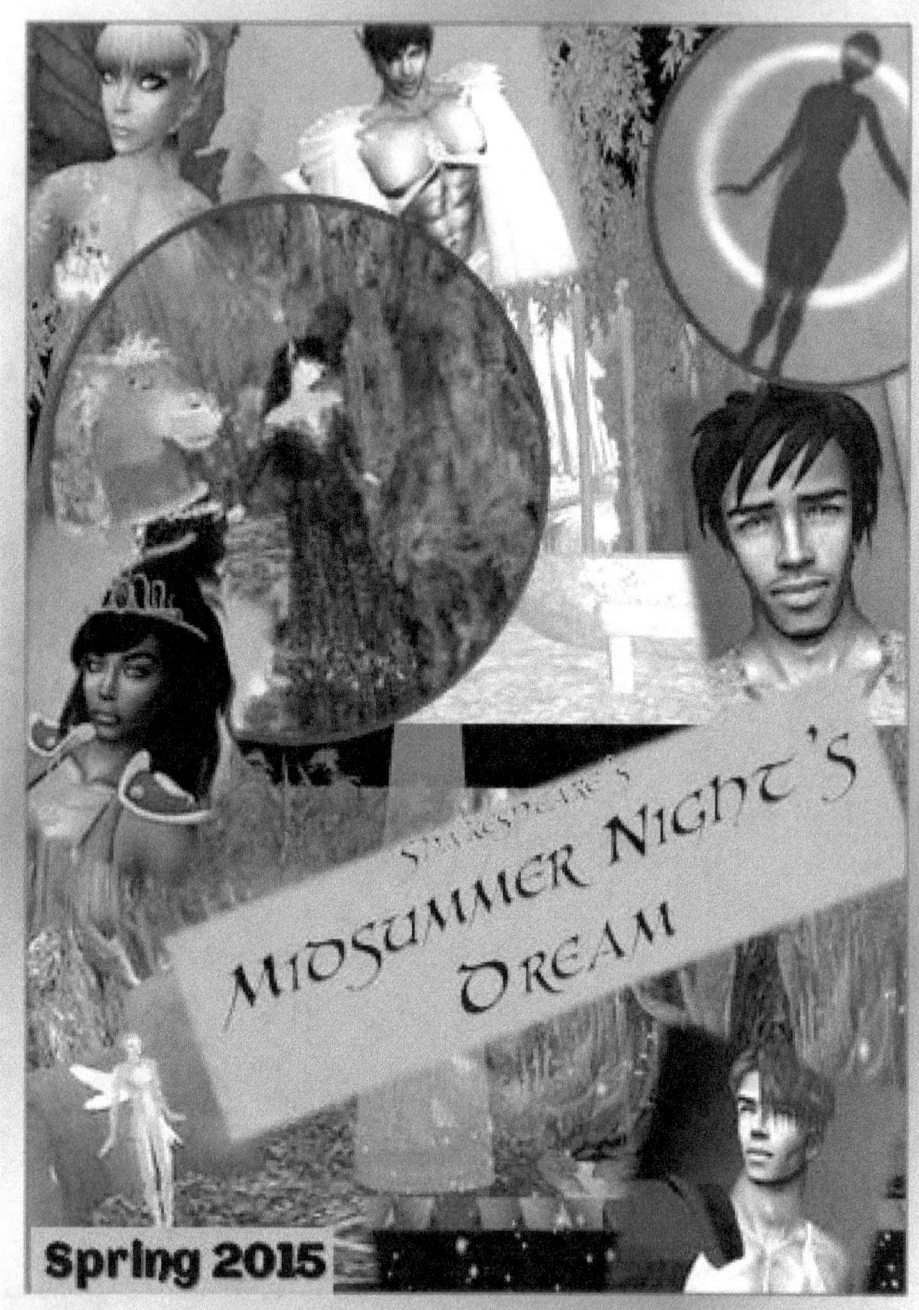

Shakespeare's
Midsummer Night's
Dream

Spring 2015

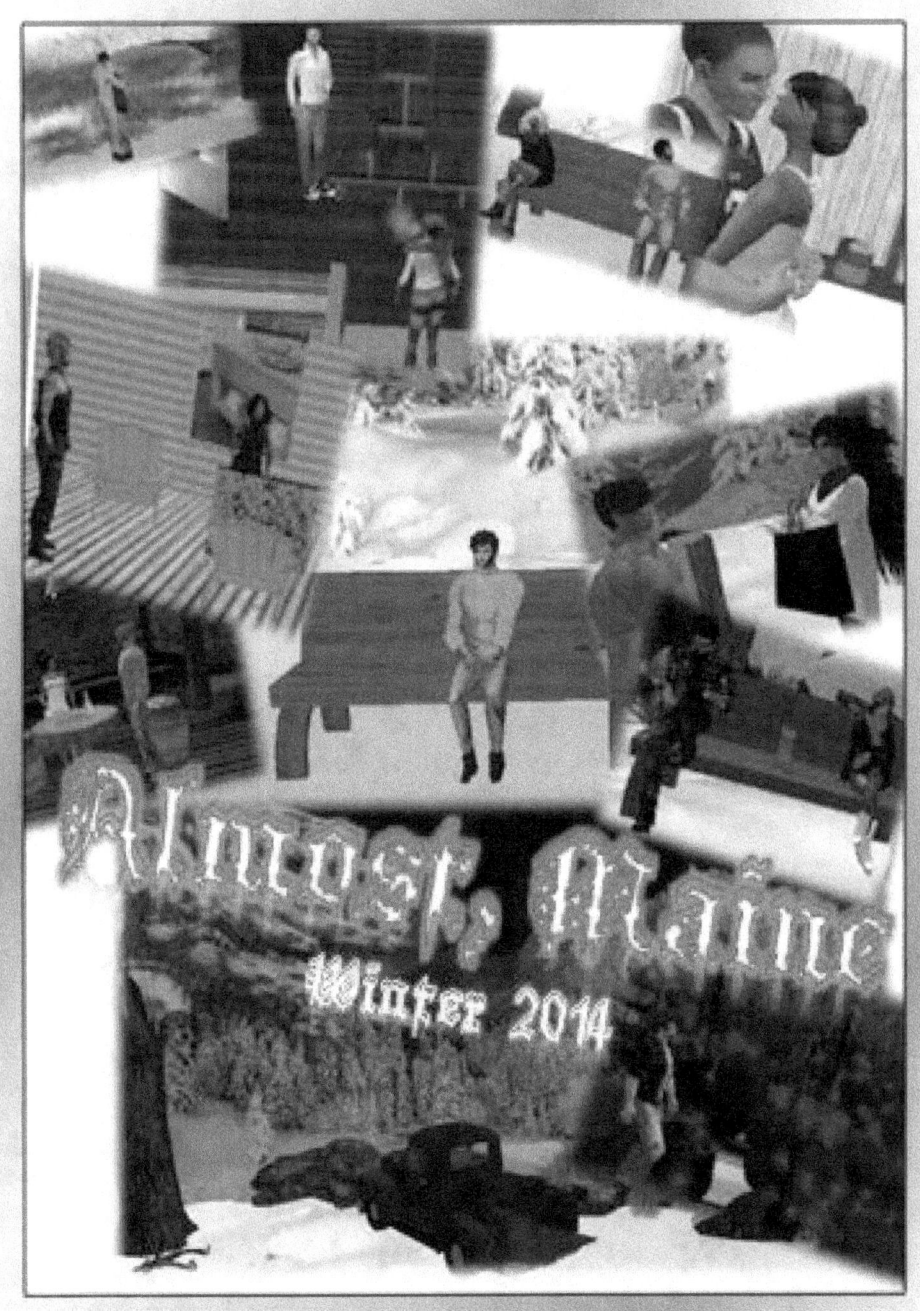

Almost Maine

Winter 2014

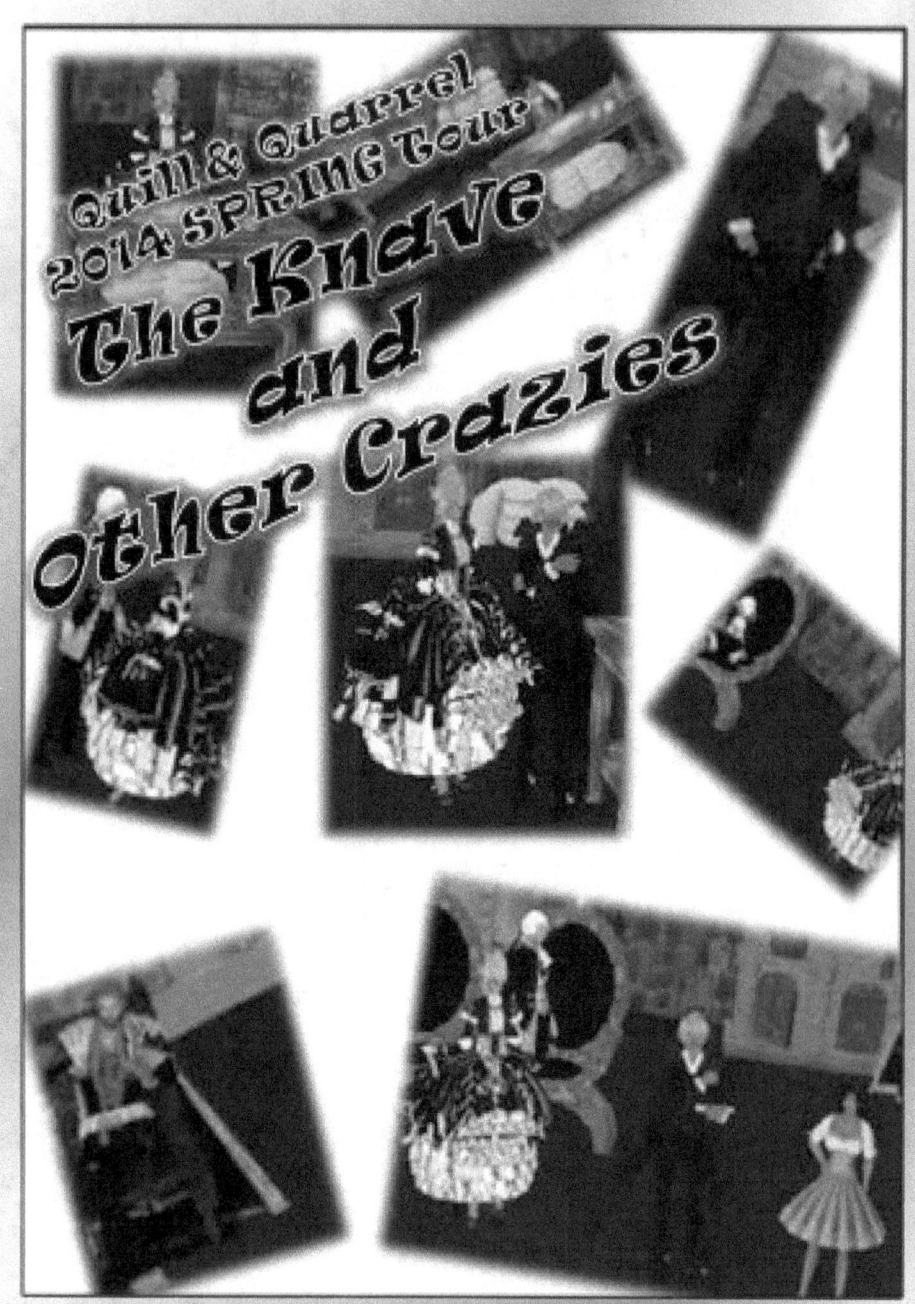

Quin & Quarrel
2014 SPRING tour
The Knave
and
Other Crazies

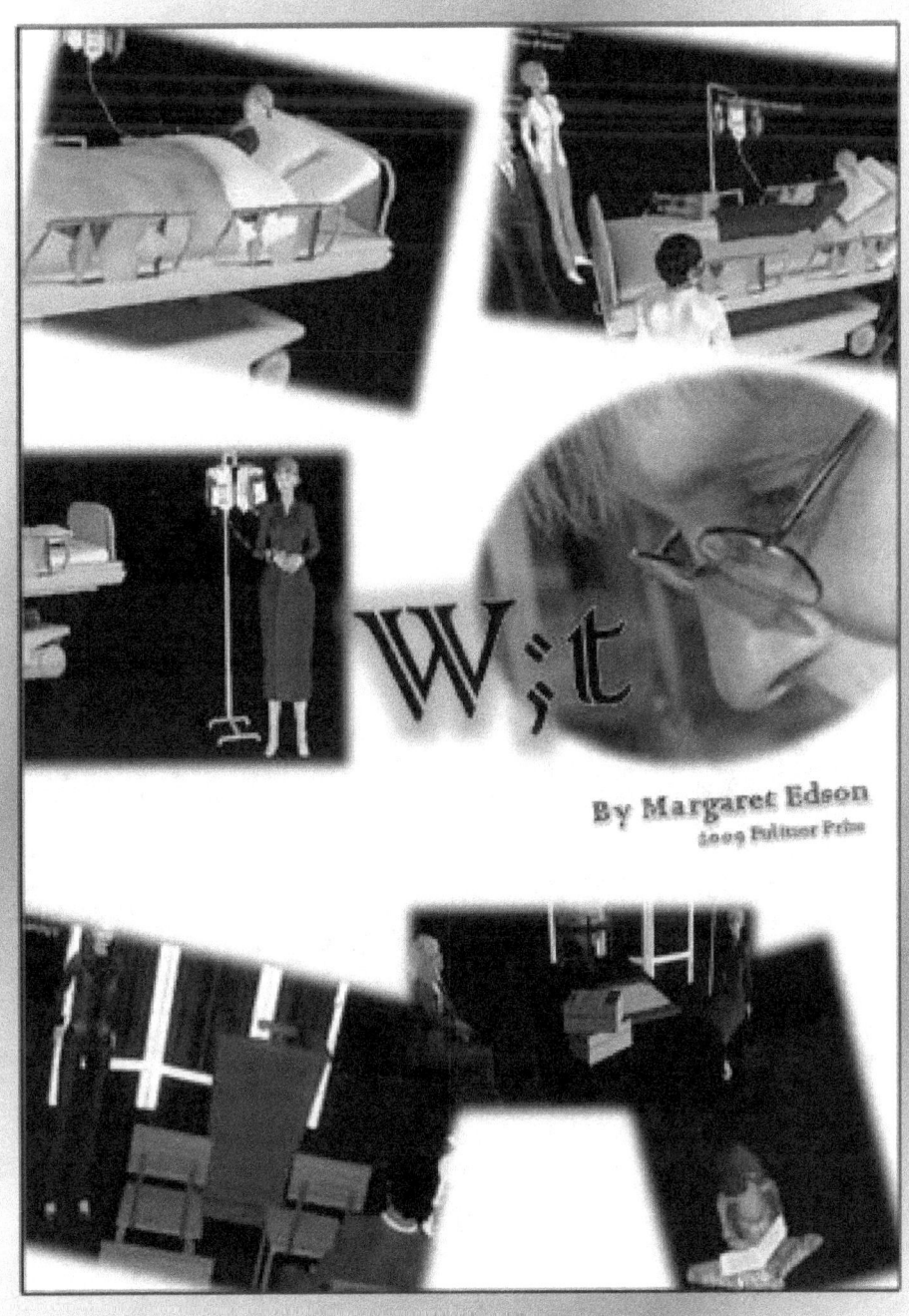

W;t

By Margaret Edson
1999 Pulitzer Prize

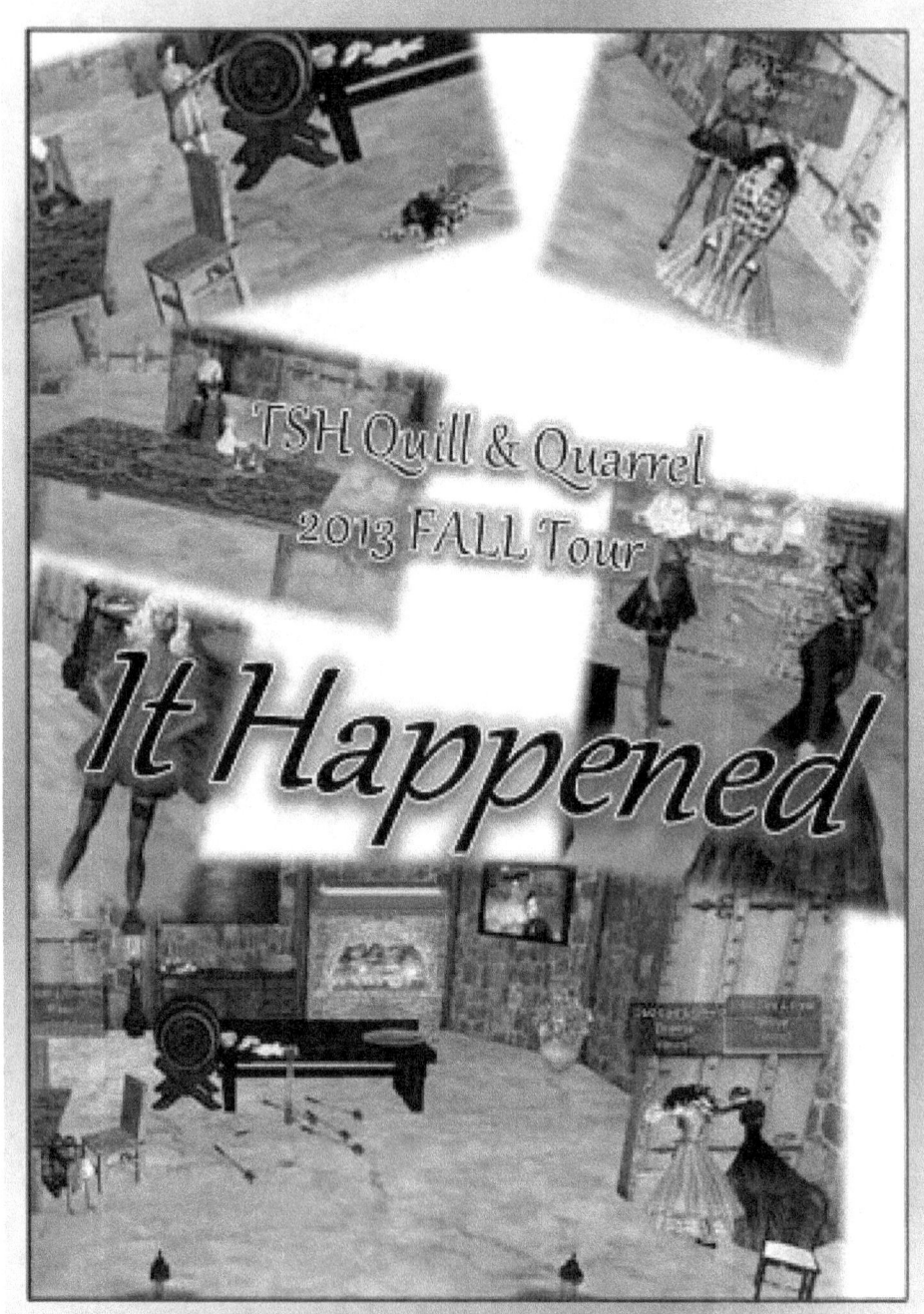

TSH Quill & Quarrel
2013 FALL Tour

It Happened

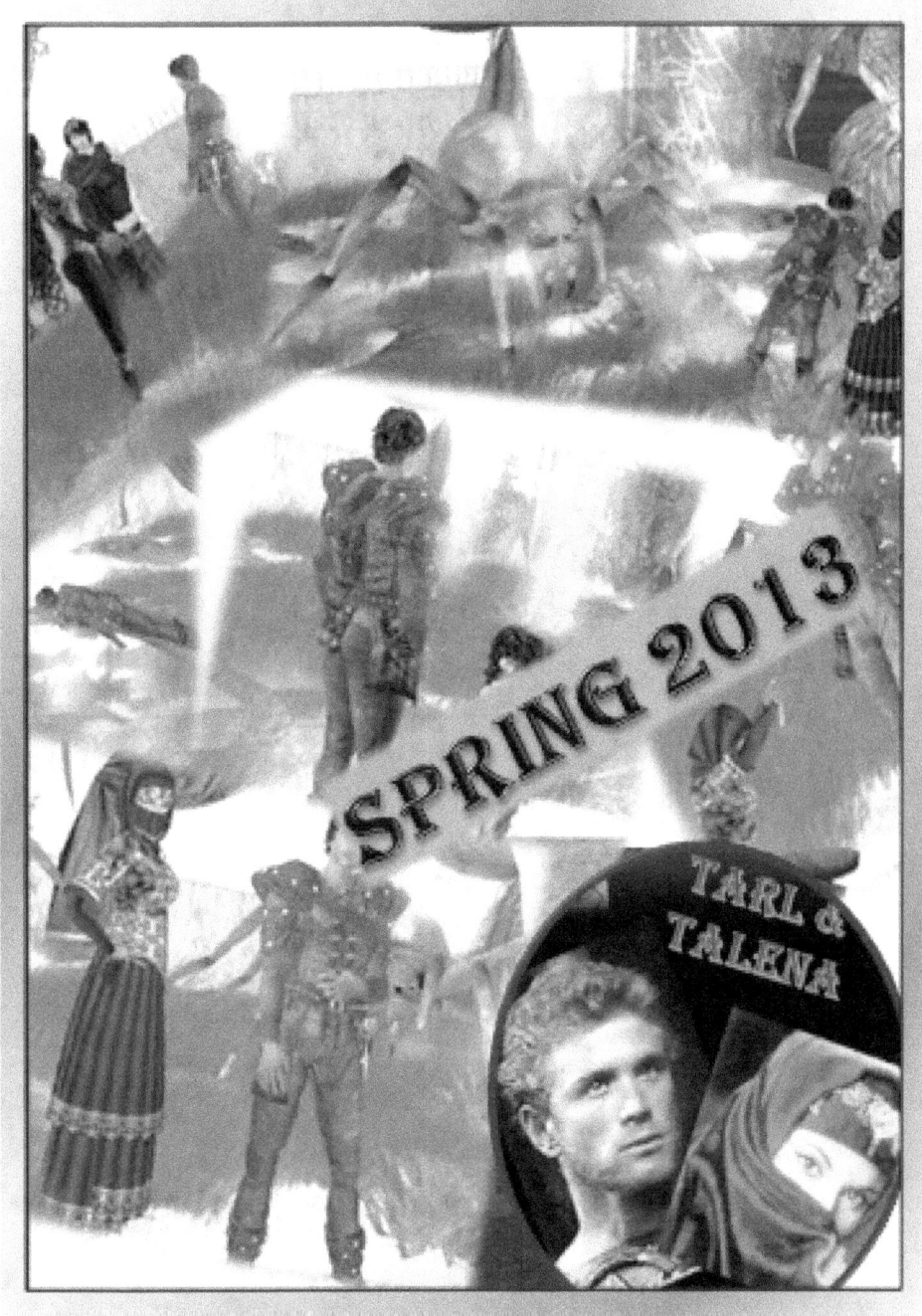

SPRING 2013

TARL & TALENA

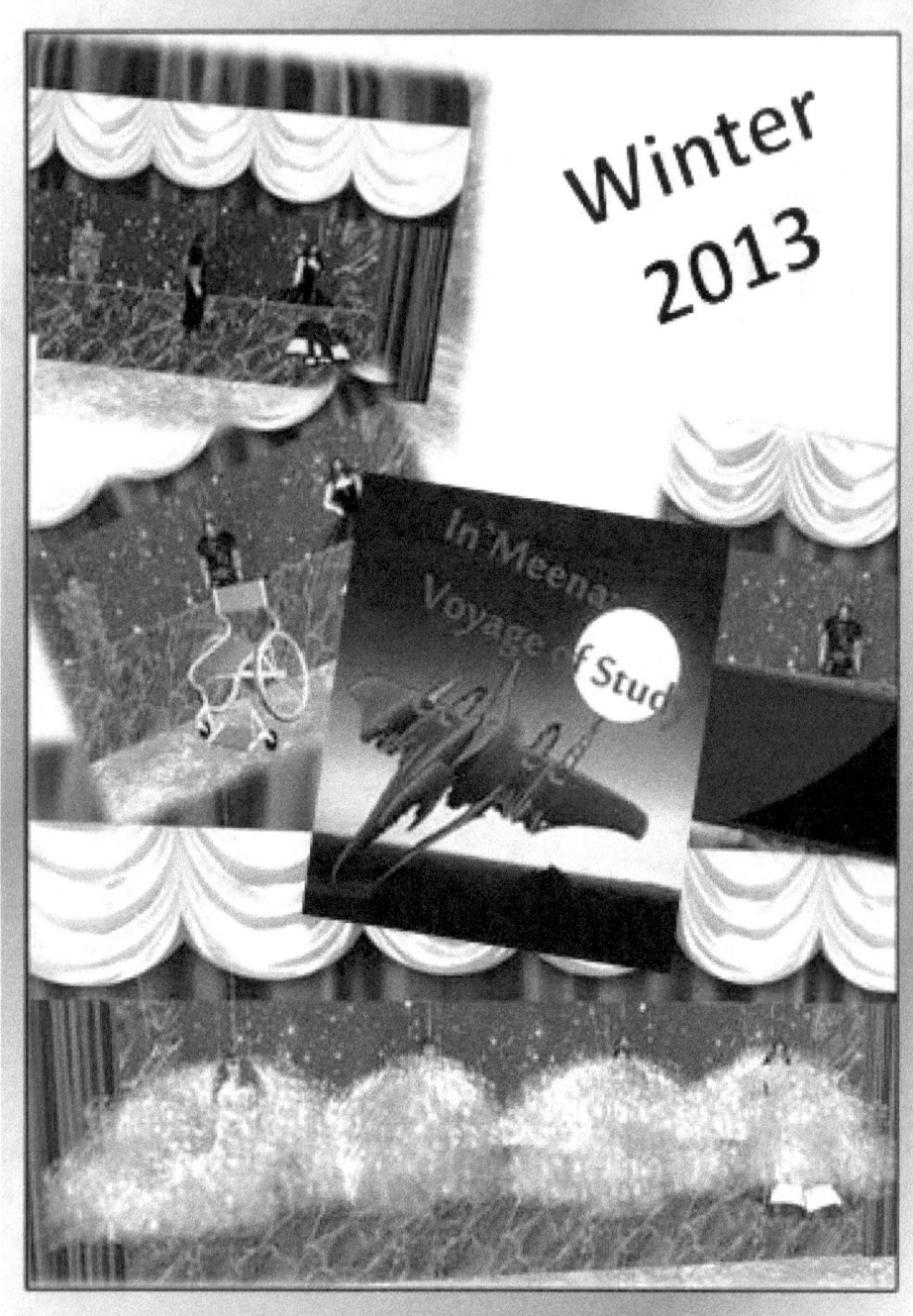

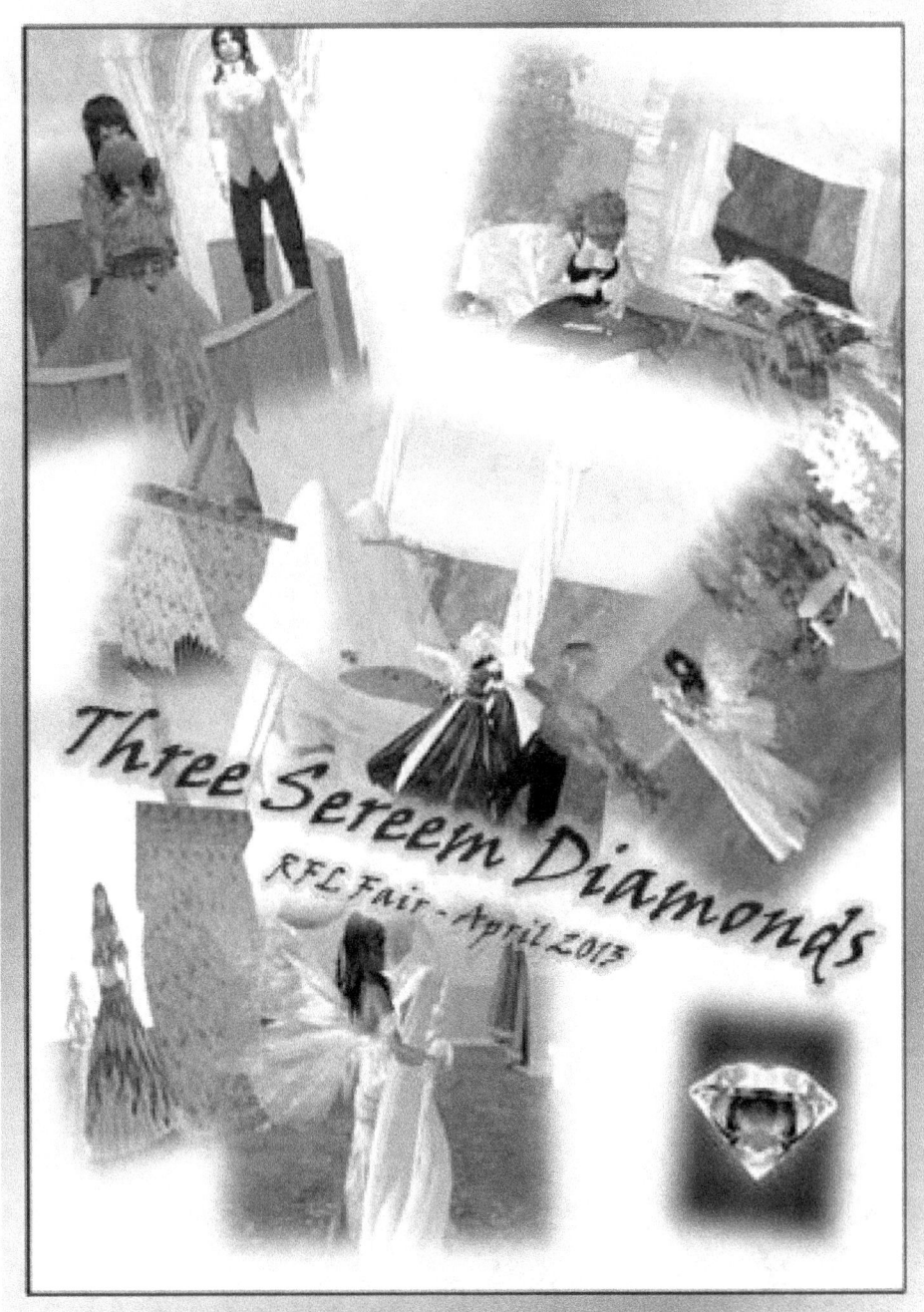

Three Sereem Diamonds
RFL Fair - April 2013

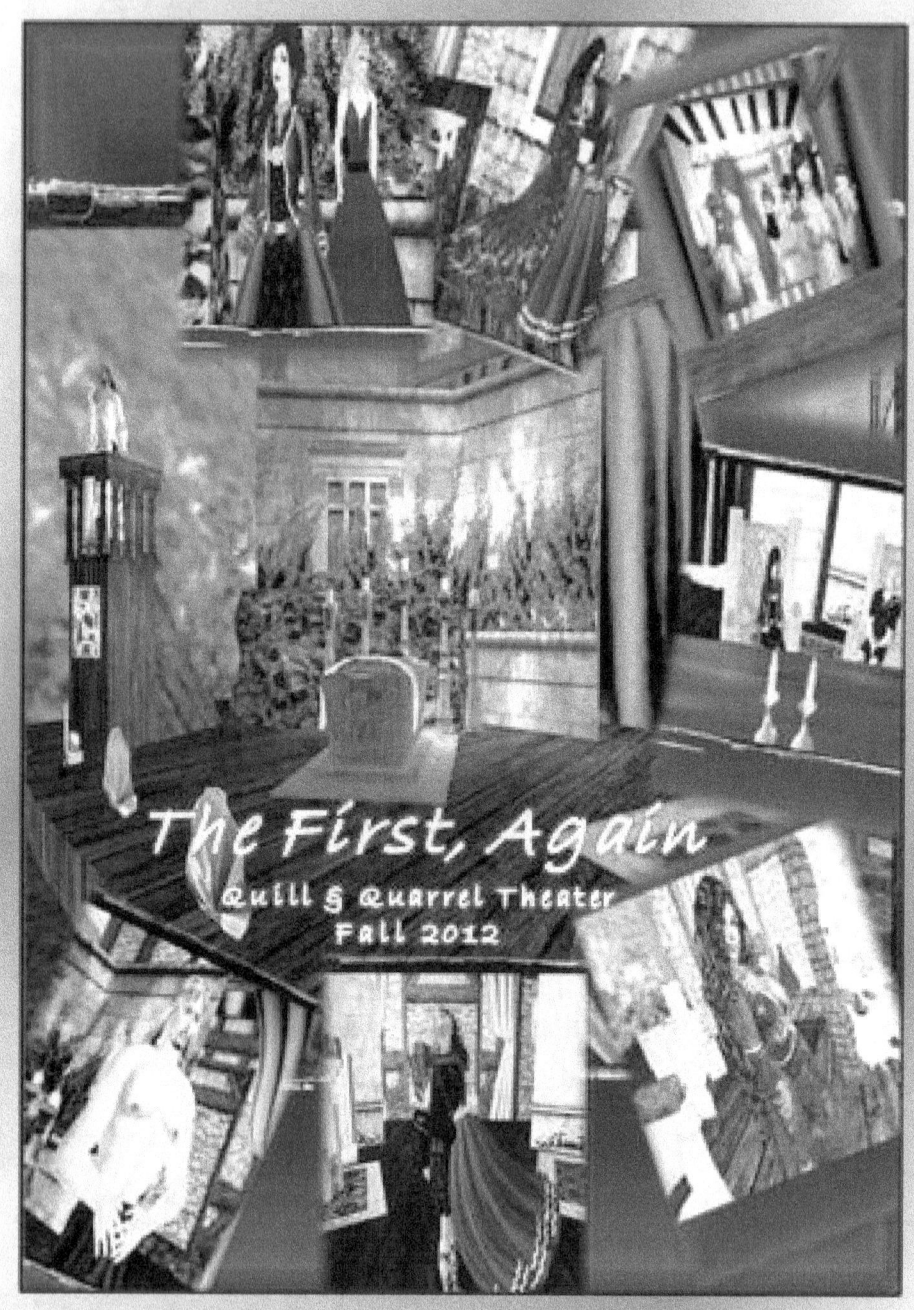

The First, Again
Quill & Quarrel Theater
Fall 2012

CURRENT PROJECTS

We have JUST learned that the Q&Q FEARLESS Theater has been awarded a Linden Endowment for the Arts Core Land Grant. This affords us the opportunity for 3 - 6 months to build, perform, and work on Linden-owned land and have their visibility and promotional power behind us.

Our goal for the use of the land is to do all we can to push the art of theater forward; we plan to start by welcoming performances there by other online performing groups.

Our hope is that by collaborating with other groups to mount shows together we can all move the art form forward and build larger audiences that we can all share.

We are hard at work preparing our Winter production "If You Remember the 60's ... You Missed the Fun!" We are putting three favorite comedy routines together on a single bill:

- Alice's Restaurant

Arlo Guthrie's musical story about Alice, and the restaurant and the Massacre on Thanksgiving Day that ultimately kept him out of the Army

- Voyage of the In'Meena

A tale of our own about four intrepid researchers who land here from far away to study Earth culture and ultimately understand almost nothing of what they see

- Nick Danger, 3rd Eye

The Firesign Theater's 'radio noir' telling of the case known as "Cut 'Em Off at the Past"

We have also selected our Spring production! We've decided to produce Oscar Wilde's "The Importance of Being Ernest".

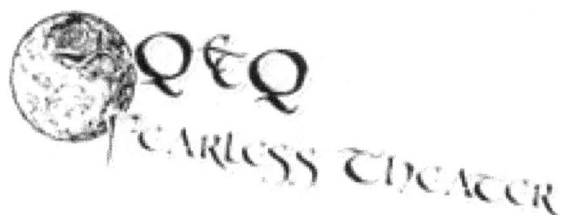

Upcoming Shows

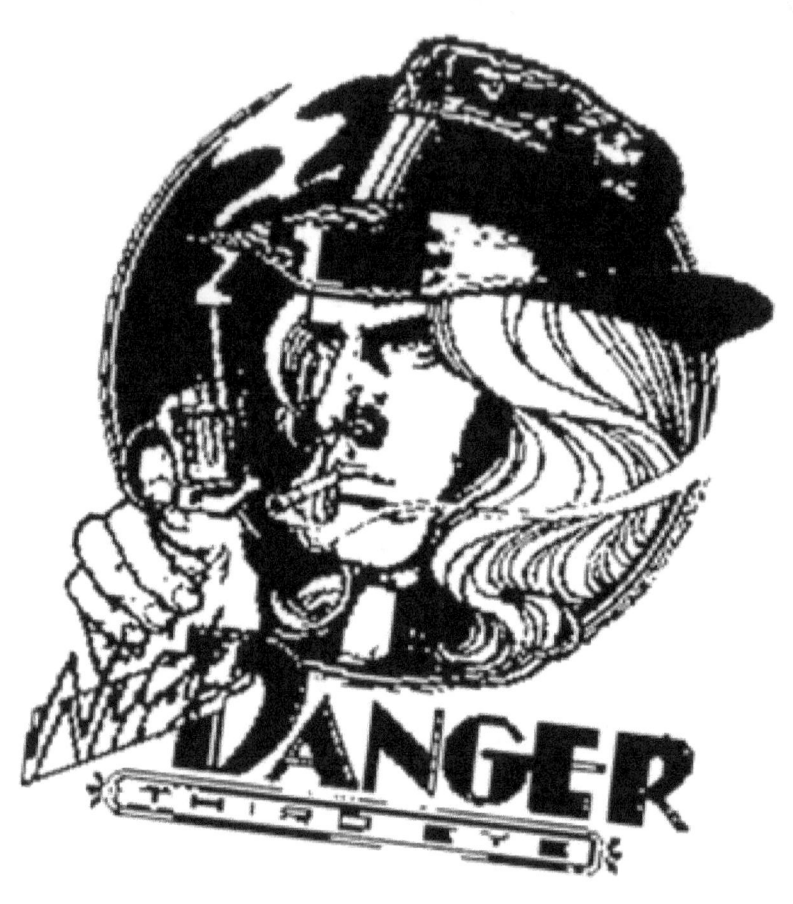

Winter 2019!

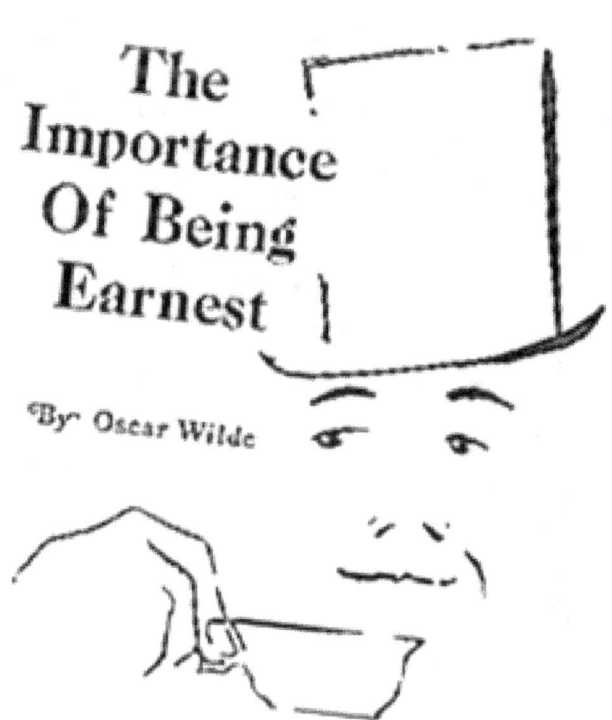

The Importance Of Being Earnest

By Oscar Wilde

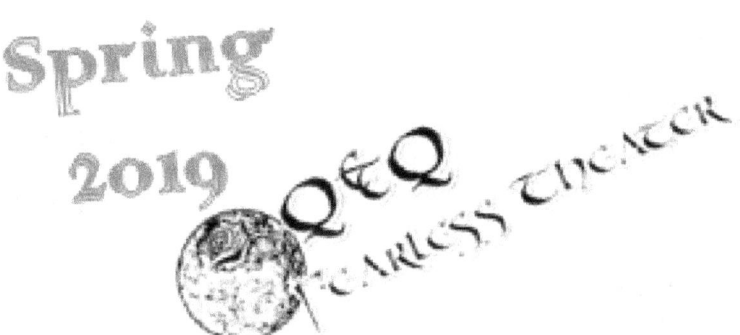

Spring 2019

QEQ FEARLESS THEATER

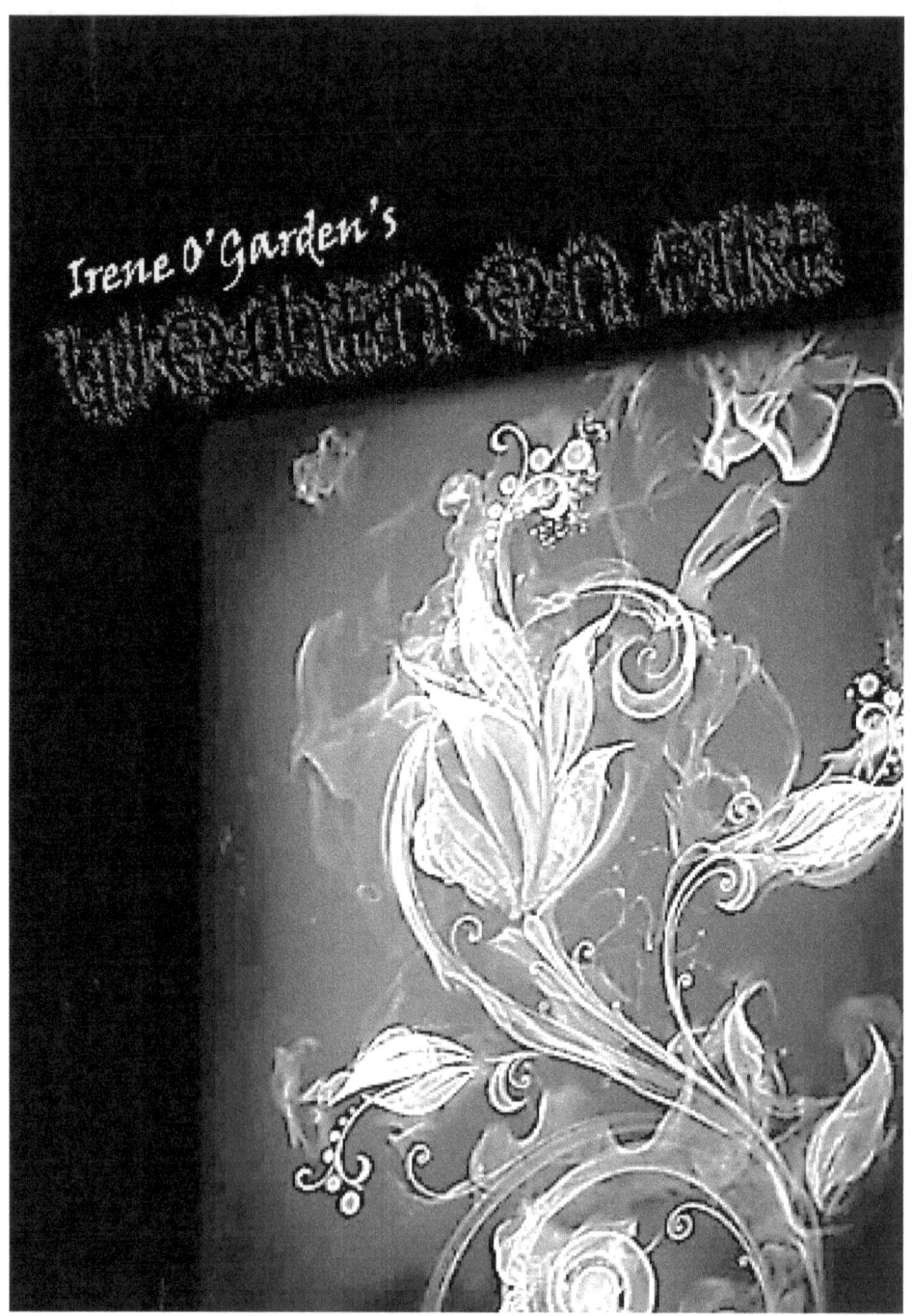

Irene O'Garden's

FUTURE VISIONS

Even after 6 years we are still able to imagine so much more than we have as yet accomplished, and, in fact, that may be the best part of the experience for us all. Our vision is what keeps us moving forward. Clearly, the electricity of live performance can't be equaled by any recording, and technology affords us the possibility of adding cinematic effects and techniques to the talents of live actors. Each new production is better than the previous one, and with each one we push the technology (and our skill in using it) beyond the edge of the envelope again.

Our next goal is to take a huge step in a new direction. We want to explore ways to present our work to a "traditional", live audience, not just to one that is online in the game platform. Some of that technology is simple enough: a sound system feed from our computer and a projector, but artistically orienting the audience and creating a unique experience for them – that is where we intend to place our main focus.

We are very excited at the prospect of giving a wider audience at least a glimpse of what is possible, and, in fact, already on its way, in the realm of live animation. We are hungry for advice, collaboration, and feedback that will push us even harder to develop our art.

Partners

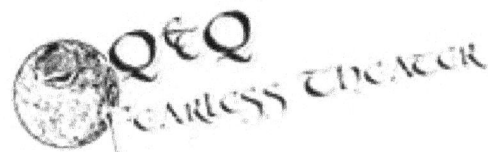

Animations and Scripting

by Taylor Schroeder [Melita]

Taylor is an accomplished actress, mistress of details and a professional programmer. There is positively no way this production would be possible without her!

She is the owner of Taylor Made - NPCs, configurable & breakable doors, LOTS of traps, RP server helper, bookcases, mailboxes, poison flowers, more!

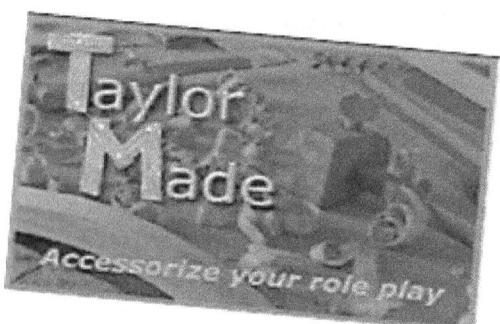

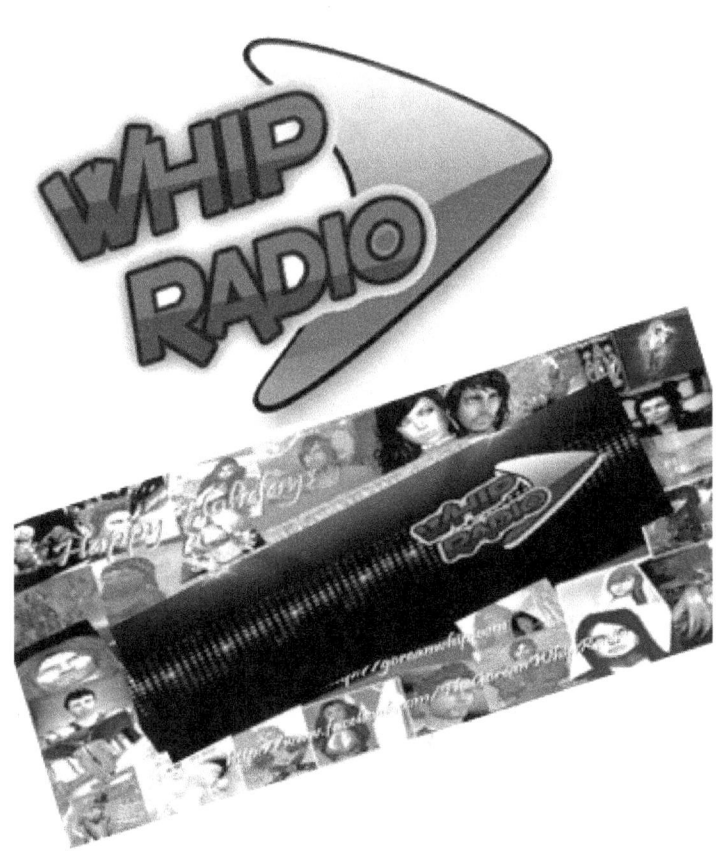

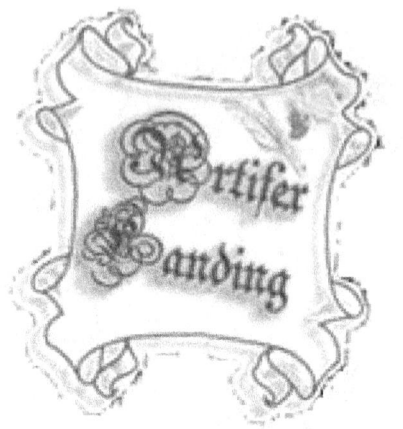

Q&Q
Arts Center

www.ingramcontent.com/pod-product-compliance
Lightning Source LLC
Chambersburg PA
CBHW071221220526
45468CB00002B/698